Ellyn Kaschak
Marcia Hill
Editors

Beyond the Rule Book: Moral Issues and Dilemmas in the Practice of Psychotherapy

Beyond the Rule Book: Moral Issues and Dilemmas in the Practice of Psychotherapy has been co-published simultaneously as *Women & Therapy,* Volume 22, Number 2 1999.

Pre-publication
REVIEWS,
COMMENTARIES,
EVALUATIONS . . .

"The authors in this important and timely book tackle the difficult task of working through . . . conflicts, sharing their moral struggles and real life solutions in working with diverse populations and in a variety of clinical settings. . . ."

Carolyn C. Larsen, PhD
Senior Counsellor Emeritus,
University of Calgary
Partner in private practice
Alberta Psychological Resources Ltd.,
Calgary
Co-editor, Ethical Decision Making in Therapy: Feminist Perspectives

Beyond the Rule Book: Moral Issues and Dilemmas in the Practice of Psychotherapy

Beyond the Rule Book: Moral Issues and Dilemmas in the Practice of Psychotherapy has been co-published simultaneously as *Women & Therapy,* Volume 22, Number 2 1999.

The *Women & Therapy* Monographic "Separates"

Below is a list of "separates," which in serials librarianship means a special issue simultaneously published as a special journal issue or double-issue *and* as a "separate" hardbound monograph. (This is a format which we also call a "DocuSerial.")

"Separates" are published because specialized libraries or professionals may wish to purchase a specific thematic issue by itself in a format which can be separately cataloged and shelved, as opposed to purchasing the journal on an on-going basis. Faculty members may also more easily consider a "separate" for classroom adoption.

"Separates" are carefully classified separately with the major book jobbers so that the journal tie-in can be noted on new book order slips to avoid duplicate purchasing.

You may wish to visit Haworth's website at . . .

http://www.haworthpressinc.com

. . . to search our online catalog for complete tables of contents of these separates and related publications.

You may also call 1-800-HAWORTH (outside US/Canada: 607-722-5857), or Fax: 1-800-895-0582 (outside US/Canada: 607-771-0012), or e-mail at:

getinfo@haworthpressinc.com

Beyond the Rule Book: Moral Issues and Dilemmas in the Practice of Psychotherapy, edited by Ellyn Kaschak, PhD, and Marcia Hill, EdD (Vol. 22, No. 2, 1999). *"The authors in this important and timely book tackle the difficult task of working through . . . conflicts, sharing their moral struggles and real life solutions in working with diverse populations and in a variety of clinical settings. . . . Will provide psychotherapists with a thought-provoking source for the stimulating and essential discussion of our own and our profession's moral bases." (Carolyn C. Larsen, PhD, Senior Counsellor Emeritus, University of Calgary, Partner in private practice, Alberta Psychological Resources Ltd., Calgary, and Co-editor, Ethical Decision Making in Therapy: Feminist Perspectives)*

Assault on the Soul: Women in the Former Yugoslavia, edited by Sara Sharratt, PhD, and Ellyn Kaschak, PhD (Vol. 22, No. 1, 1999). *Explores the applications and intersections of feminist therapy, activism and jurisprudence with women and children in the former Yugoslavia.*

Learning from Our Mistakes: Difficulties and Failures in Feminist Therapy, edited by Marcia Hill, EdD, and Esther D. Rothblum, PhD (Vol. 21, No. 3, 1998). *"A courageous and fundamental step in evolving a well-grounded body of theory and of investigating the assumptions that unexamined, lead us to error." (Teresa Bernardez, MD, Training and Supervising Analyst, The Michigan Psychoanalytic Council)*

Feminist Therapy as a Political Act, edited by Marcia Hill, EdD (Vol. 21, No. 2, 1998). *"A real contribution to the field. . . . A valuable tool for feminist therapists and those who want to learn about feminist therapy." (Florence L. Denmark, PhD, Robert S. Pace Distinguished Professor of Psychology and Chair, Psychology Department, Pace University, New York, New York)*

Breaking the Rules: Women in Prison and Feminist Therapy, edited by Judy Harden, PhD, and Marcia Hill, EdD (Vol. 20, No. 4 & Vol. 21, No. 1, 1998). *"Fills a long-recognized gap in the psychology of women curricula, demonstrating that feminist theory can be made relevant to the practice of feminism, even in prison." (Suzanne J. Kessler, PhD, Professor of Psychology and Women's Studies, State University of New York at Purchase)*

Children's Rights, Therapists' Responsibilities: Feminist Commentaries, edited by Gail Anderson, MA, and Marcia Hill, EdD (Vol. 20, No. 2, 1997). *"Addresses specific practice dimensions that will help therapists organize and resolve conflicts about working with children, adolescents, and their families in therapy." (Feminist Bookstore News)*

More than a Mirror: How Clients Influence Therapists' Lives, edited by Marcia Hill, EdD (Vol. 20, No. 1, 1997). *"Courageous, insightful, and deeply moving. These pages reveal the scrupulous self-examination* *and self-reflection of conscientious therapists at their best. AN IMPORTANT CONTRIBUTION TO FEMINIST THERAPY LITERATURE AND A BOOK WORTH READING BY THERAPISTS AND CLIENTS ALIKE." (Rachel Josefowitz Siegal, MSW, retired feminist therapy practitioner; Co-Editor, Women Changing Therapy; Jewish Women in Therapy; and Celebrating the Lives of Jewish Women: Patterns in a Feminist Sampler)*

Sexualities, edited by Marny Hall, PhD, LCSW (Vol. 19, No. 4, 1997). *"Explores the diverse and multifaceted nature of female sexuality, covering topics including sadomasochism in the therapy room, sexual exploitation in cults, and genderbending in cyberspace." (Feminist Bookstore News)*

Couples Therapy: Feminist Perspectives, edited by Marcia Hill, EdD, and Esther D. Rothblum, PhD (Vol. 19, No. 3, 1996). *Addresses some of the inadequacies, omissions, and assumptions in traditional couples' therapy to help you face the issues of race, ethnicity, and sexual orientation in helping couples today.*

A Feminist Clinician's Guide to the Memory Debate, edited by Susan Contratto, PhD, and M. Janice Gutfreund, PhD (Vol. 19, No. 1, 1996). *"Unites diverse scholars, clinicians, and activists in an insightful and useful examination of the issues related to recovered memories." (Feminist Bookstore News)*

Classism and Feminist Therapy: Counting Costs, edited by Marcia Hill, EdD, and Esther D. Rothblum, PhD (Vol. 18, No. 3/4, 1996). *"EDUCATES, CHALLENGES, AND QUESTIONS THE INFLUENCE OF CLASSISM ON THE CLINICAL PRACTICE OF PSYCHOTHERAPY WITH WOMEN." (Kathleen P. Gates, MA, Certified Professional Counselor, Center for Psychological Health, Superior, Wisconsin)*

Lesbian Therapists and Their Therapy: From Both Sides of the Couch, edited by Nancy D. Davis, MD, Ellen Cole, PhD, and Esther D. Rothblum, PhD (Vol. 18, No. 2, 1996). *"Highlights the power and boundary issues of psychotherapy from perspectives that many readers may have neither considered nor experienced in their own professional lives." (Psychiatric Services)*

Feminist Foremothers in Women's Studies, Psychology, and Mental Health, edited by Phyllis Chesler, PhD, Esther D. Rothblum, PhD, and Ellen Cole, PhD (Vol. 17, No. 1/2/3/4, 1995). *"A must for feminist scholars and teachers . . . These women's personal experiences are poignant and powerful." (Women's Studies International Forum)*

Women's Spirituality, Women's Lives, edited by Judith Ochshorn, PhD, and Ellen Cole, PhD (Vol. 16, No. 2/3, 1995). *"A delightful and complex book on spirituality and sacredness in women's lives." (Joan Clingan, MA, Spiritual Psychology, Graduate Advisor, Prescott College Master of Arts Program)*

Psychopharmacology from a Feminist Perspective, edited by Jean A. Hamilton, MD, Margaret Jensvold, MD, Esther D. Rothblum, PhD, and Ellen Cole, PhD (Vol. 16, No. 1, 1995). *"Challenges readers to increase their sensitivity and awareness of the role of sex and gender in response to and acceptance of pharmacologic therapy." (American Journal of Pharmaceutical Education)*

Wilderness Therapy for Women: The Power of Adventure, edited by Ellen Cole, PhD, Esther D. Rothblum, PhD, and Eve Erdman, MEd, MLS (Vol. 15, No. 3/4, 1994). *"There's an undeniable excitement in these pages about the thrilling satisfaction of meeting challenges in the physical world, the world outside our cities that is unfamiliar, uneasy territory for many women. If you're interested at all in the subject, this book is well worth your time." (Psychology of Women Quarterly)*

Bringing Ethics Alive: Feminist Ethics in Psychotherapy Practice, edited by Nanette K. Gartrell, MD (Vol. 15, No. 1, 1994). *"Examines the theoretical and practical issues of ethics in feminist therapies. From the responsibilities of training programs to include social issues ranging from racism to sexism to practice ethics, this outlines real questions and concerns." (Midwest Book Review)*

Women with Disabilities: Found Voices, edited by Mary Willmuth, PhD, and Lillian Holcomb, PhD (Vol. 14, No. 3/4, 1994). *"These powerful chapters often jolt the anti-disability consciousness and force readers to contend with the ways in which disability has been constructed, disguised, and rendered disgusting by much of society." (Academic Library Book Review)*

Faces of Women and Aging, edited by Nancy D. Davis, MD, Ellen Cole, PhD, and Esther D. Rothblum, PhD (Vol. 14, No. 1/2, 1993). *"This uplifting, helpful book is of great value not only for aging* *women, but also for women of all ages who are interested in taking active control of their own lives." (New Mature Woman)*

Refugee Women and Their Mental Health: Shattered Societies, Shattered Lives, edited by Ellen Cole, PhD, Oliva M. Espin, PhD, and Esther D. Rothblum, PhD (Vol. 13, No. 1/2/3, 1992). *"The ideas presented are rich and the perspectives varied, and the book is an important contribution to understanding refugee women in a global context." (Comtemporary Psychology)*

Women, Girls and Psychotherapy: Reframing Resistance, edited by Carol Gilligan, PhD, Annie Rogers, PhD, and Deborah Tolman, EdD (Vol. 11, No. 3/4, 1991). *"Of use to educators, psychotherapists, and parents–in short, to any person who is directly involved with girls at adolescence." (Harvard Educational Review)*

Professional Training for Feminist Therapists: Personal Memoirs, edited by Esther D. Rothblum, PhD, and Ellen Cole, PhD (Vol. 11, No. 1, 1991). *"Exciting, interesting, and filled with the angst and the energies that directed these women to develop an entirely different approach to counseling." (Science Books & Films)*

Jewish Women in Therapy: Seen But Not Heard, edited by Rachel Josefowitz Siegel, MSW, and Ellen Cole, PhD (Vol. 10, No. 4, 1991). *"A varied collection of prose and poetry, first-person stories, and accessible theoretical pieces that can help Jews and non-Jews, women and men, therapists and patients, and general readers to grapple with questions of Jewish women's identities and diversity." (Canadian Psychology)*

Women's Mental Health in Africa, edited by Esther D. Rothblum, PhD, and Ellen Cole, PhD (Vol. 10, No. 3, 1990). *"A valuable contribution and will be of particular interest to scholars in women's studies, mental health, and cross-cultural psychology." (Contemporary Psychology)*

Motherhood: A Feminist Perspective, edited by Jane Price Knowles, MD, and Ellen Cole, PhD (Vol. 10, No. 1/2, 1990). *"Provides some enlightening perspectives. . . . It is worth the time of both male and female readers." (Comtemporary Psychology)*

Diversity and Complexity in Feminist Therapy, edited by Laura Brown, PhD, ABPP, and Maria P. P. Root, PhD (Vol. 9, No. 1/2, 1990). *"A most convincing discussion and illustration of the importance of adopting a multicultural perspective for theory building in feminist therapy. . . . THIS BOOK IS A MUST FOR THERAPISTS and should be included on psychology of women syllabi." (Association for Women in Psychology Newsletter)*

Fat Opression and Psychotherapy, edited by Laura S. Brown, PhD, and Esther D. Rothblum, PhD (Vol. 8, No. 3, 1990). *"Challenges many traditional beliefs about being fat . . . A refreshing new perspective for approaching and thinking about issues related to weight." (Association for Women in Psychology Newsletter)*

Lesbianism: Affirming Nontraditional Roles, edited by Esther D. Rothblum, PhD, and Ellen Cole, PhD (Vol. 8, No. 1/2, 1989). *"Touches on many of the most significant issues brought before therapists today." (Newsletter of the Association of Gay & Lesbian Psychiatrists)*

Women and Sex Therapy: Closing the Circle of Sexual Knowledge, edited by Ellen Cole, PhD, and Esther D. Rothblum, PhD (Vol. 7, No. 2/3, 1989). *"ADDS IMMEASUREABLY TO THE FEMINIST THERAPY LITERATURE THAT DISPELS MALE PARADIGMS OF PATHOLOGY WITH REGARD TO WOMEN." (Journal of Sex Education & Therapy)*

The Politics of Race and Gender in Therapy, edited by Lenora Fulani, PhD (Vol. 6, No. 4, 1988). *Women of color examine newer therapies that encourage them to develop their historical identity.*

Treating Women's Fear of Failure, edited by Esther D. Rothblum, PhD, and Ellen Cole, PhD (Vol. 6, No. 3, 1988). *"SHOULD BE RECOMMENDED READING FOR ALL MENTAL HEALTH PROFESSIONALS, SOCIAL WORKERS, EDUCATORS, AND VOCATIONAL COUNSELORS WHO WORK WITH WOMEN." (The Journal of Clinical Psychiatry)*

Women, Power, and Therapy: Issues for Women, edited by Marjorie Braude, MD (Vol. 6, No. 1/2, 1987). *"RAISE[S] THERAPISTS' CONSCIOUSNESS ABOUT THE IMPORTANCE OF CONSIDERING GENDER-BASED POWER IN THERAPY. . . welcome contribution." (Australian Journal of Psychology)*

Dynamics of Feminist Therapy, edited by Doris Howard (Vol. 5, No. 2/3, 1987). *"A comprehensive treatment of an important and vexing subject." (Australian Journal of Sex, Marriage and Family)*

A Woman's Recovery from the Trauma of War: Twelve Responses from Feminist Therapists and Activists, edited by Esther D. Rothblum, PhD, and Ellen Cole, PhD (Vol. 5, No. 1, 1986). *"A MILESTONE. In it, twelve women pay very close attention to a woman who has been deeply wounded by war." (The World)*

Women and Mental Health: New Directions for Change, edited by Carol T. Mowbray, PhD, Susan Lanir, MA, and Marilyn Hulce, MSW, ACSW (Vol. 3, No. 3/4, 1985). *"The overview of sex differences in disorders is clear and sensitive, as is the review of sexual exploitation of clients by therapists. . . . MANDATORY READING FOR ALL THERAPISTS WHO WORK WITH WOMEN." (British Journal of Medical Psychology and The British Psychological Society)*

Women Changing Therapy: New Assessments, Values, and Strategies in Feminist Therapy, edited by Joan Hamerman Robbins and Rachel Josefowitz Siegel, MSW (Vol. 2, No. 2/3, 1983). *"An excellent collection to use in teaching therapists that reflection and resolution in treatment do not simply lead tp adaptation, but to an active inner process of judging." (News for Women in Psychiatry)*

Current Feminist Issues in Psychotherapy, edited by The New England Association for Women in Psychology (Vol. 1, No. 3, 1983). *Addresses depression, displaced homemakers, sibling incest, and body image from a feminist perspective.*

∞ ALL HAWORTH BOOKS AND JOURNALS ARE PRINTED ON CERTIFIED ACID-FREE PAPER

Beyond the Rule Book: Moral Issues and Dilemmas in the Practice of Psychotherapy

Ellyn Kaschak, PhD
Marcia Hill, EdD
Editors

Beyond the Rule Book: Moral Issues and Dilemmas in the Practice of Psychotherapy has been co-published simultaneously as *Women & Therapy,* Volume 22, Number 2 1999.

The Haworth Press, Inc.
New York • London • Oxford

Beyond the Rule Book: Moral Issues and Dilemmas in the Practice of Psychotherapy has been co-published simultaneously as *Women & Therapy*™, Volume 22, Number 2 1999.

© 1999 by The Haworth Press, Inc. All rights reserved. No part of this work may be reproduced or utilized in any form or by any means, electronic or mechanical, including photocopying, microfilm and recording, or by any information storage and retrieval system, without permission in writing from the publisher. Printed in the United States of America.

The development, preparation, and publication of this work has been undertaken with great care. However, the publisher, employees, editors, and agents of The Haworth Press and all imprints of The Haworth Press, Inc., including The Haworth Medical Press® and Pharmaceutical Products Press®, are not responsible for any errors contained herein or for consequences that may ensue from use of materials or information contained in this work. Opinions expressed by the author(s) are not necessarily those of The Haworth Press, Inc.

The Haworth Press, Inc., 10 Alice Street, Binghamton, NY 13904-1580 USA

Cover design by Thomas J. Mayshock Jr.

Library of Congress Cataloging-in-Publication Data

Beyond the rule book : moral issues and dilemmas in the practice of psychotherapy / Ellyn Kaschak, Marcia Hill, editors.
    p. cm.
   "Co-published simultaneously as Women & therapy, volume 22, number 2 1999."
   Includes bibliographical references and index.
   ISBN 0-7890-0772-X (alk. paper). – ISBN 0-7890-0773-8 (alk. paper)
   1. Feminist therapy–Moral and ethical aspects. I. Kaschak, Ellyn, 1943- . II. Hill, Marcia.
RC489.F45B49 1999
616.89′14–dc21   99-33952
                                                                                                         CIP

INDEXING & ABSTRACTING

Contributions to this publication are selectively indexed or abstracted in print, electronic, online, or CD-ROM version(s) of the reference tools and information services listed below. This list is current as of the copyright date of this publication. See the end of this section for additional notes.

- *Abstracts of Research in Pastoral Care & Counseling*
- *Academic Abstracts/CD-ROM*
- *Academic Index (on-line)*
- *Alternative Press Index*
- *Behavioral Medicine Abstracts*
- *BUBL Information Service, an Internet-based Information Service for the UK higher education community*
- *CNPIEC Reference Guide: Chinese National Directory of Foreign Periodicals*
- *Contemporary Women's Issues*
- *Current Contents: Clinical Medicine/Life Sciences (CC: CM/LS) (weekly Table of Contents Service), and Social Science Citation Index. Articles also searchable through Social SciSearch, ISI's online database and in ISI's Research Alert current awareness service*
- *Digest of Neurology and Psychiatry*
- *Expanded Academic Index*
- *Family Studies Database (online and CD/ROM)*
- *Family Violence & Sexual Assault Bulletin*
- *Feminist Periodicals: A Current Listing of Contents*
- *GenderWatch*
- *Health Source: Indexing & Abstracting of 160 selected health related journals, updated monthly*

(continued)

- *Health Source Plus: expanded version of "Health Source" to be released shortly*
- *Higher Education Abstracts*
- *IBZ International Bibliography of Periodical Literature*
- *Index to Periodical Articles Related to Law*
- *Mental Health Abstracts (online through DIALOG)*
- *ONS Nursing Scan in Oncology-NAACOG's Women's Health Nursing Scan*
- *PASCAL, c/o Institute de L'Information Scientifique et Technique. Cross-disciplinary electronic database covering the fields of science, technology & medicine. Also available on CD-ROM.*
- *Periodical Abstracts, Research I, general & basic reference indexing & abstracting data-base from University Microfilms International (UMI)*
- *Periodical Abstracts, Research II, broad coverage indexing & abstracting data-base from University Microfilms International (UMI)*
- *Psychological Abstracts (PsycINFO)*
- *Published International Literature on Traumatic Stress (The PILOTS Database)*
- *Sage Family Studies Abstracts (SFSA)*
- *Social Work Abstracts*
- *Sociological Abstracts (SA)*
- *Studies on Women Abstracts*
- *Violence and Abuse Abstracts: A Review of Current Literature on Interpersonal Violence (VAA)*
- *Women Studies Abstracts*
- *Women's Studies Index (indexed comprehensively)*

(continued)

*Special Bibliographic Notes related to special journal issues
(separates) and indexing/abstracting:*

- indexing/abstracting services in this list will also cover material in any "separate" that is co-published simultaneously with Haworth's special thematic journal issue or DocuSerial. Indexing/abstracting usually covers material at the article/chapter level.
- monographic co-editions are intended for either non-subscribers or libraries which intend to purchase a second copy for their circulating collections.
- monographic co-editions are reported to all jobbers/wholesalers/approval plans. The source journal is listed as the "series" to assist the prevention of duplicate purchasing in the same manner utilized for books-in-series.
- to facilitate user/access services all indexing/abstracting services are encouraged to utilize the co-indexing entry note indicated at the bottom of the first page of each article/chapter/contribution.
- this is intended to assist a library user of any reference tool (whether print, electronic, online, or CD-ROM) to locate the monographic version if the library has purchased this version but not a subscription to the source journal.
- individual articles/chapters in any Haworth publication are also available through the Haworth Document Delivery Service (HDDS).

ABOUT THE EDITORS

Ellyn Kaschak, PhD, is Professor of Psychology at San Jose State University in San Jose, California. She is author of *Engendered Lives: A New Psychology of Women's Experience*, as well as numerous articles and chapters on feminist psychology and psychotherapy. She has had thirty years of experience practicing psychotherapy, is past Chair of the Feminist Therapy Institute and of the APA Committee on Women and is Fellow of Division 35, the Psychology of Women, Division 12, Clinical Psychology, Division 45, Ethnic Minority Issues and Division 50, International Psychology, of the American Psychological Association. She is co-editor of the journal *Women & Therapy*.

Marcia Hill, EdD, is a psychologist who has spent over 25 years practicing psychotherapy. She is co-editor of the journal *Women & Therapy* and a member and past Chair of the Feminist Therapy Institute. In addition to therapy, Dr. Hill does occasional teaching, writing, and consulting in the areas of feminist therapy theory and practice. The Editor of *More than a Mirror: How Clients Influence Therapists' Lives* (1997) and *Feminist Therapy as a Political Act* (1998), she has co-edited five other Haworth books: *Classism and Feminist Therapy: Counting Costs* (1996); *Couples Therapy: Feminist Perspectives* (1996); *Children's Rights, Therapists' Responsibilities: Feminist Commentaries* (1997); *Breaking the Rules: Women in Prison and Feminist Therapy* (1998) and *Learning from Our Mistakes: Difficulties and Failures in Feminist Therapy* (1999). She is currently in private practice in Montpelier, Vermont.

Beyond the Rule Book:
Moral Issues and Dilemmas
in the Practice of Psychotherapy

CONTENTS

Beyond the Rule Book   1
Ellyn Kaschak

The Ostrich Raises Its Head: "Knowing" and Moral
   Accountability in the Practice of Psychotherapy   7
Alexandra Bloom

The Politics of Naming and the Development of Morality:
   Implications for Feminist Therapists   21
Gayle E. Pitman

What Is Necessary, and What Is Right? Feminist Dilemmas
   in Community Mental Health   39
Lynda L. Warwick

Fragmentation and Integrity: The Search
   for a Moral Compass While Working as a Therapist
   Within the Child Welfare System   53
Sharla Kibel

In the Belly of the Beast: Morals, Ethics,
   and Feminist Psychotherapy with Women in Prison   69
Cindy M. Bruns
Teresa M. Lesko

The Personal, Professional and Political
   When Clients Have Disabilities   87
Rhoda Olkin

Morality and Responsibility: Necessary Components
   of Feminist Therapy   105
      Kayla Miriyam Weiner

Split Loyalties: The Conflicting Demands of Individual
   Treatment Goals and Parental Responsibility   117
      Sally A. Keller

The Moral Imperative: Self-Care for Women Psychotherapists   133
      Lynne Carroll
      Paula J. Gilroy
      Jennifer Murra

Index   145

Beyond the Rule Book

No human relationship can exist outside a moral framework, whether that framework is considered to derive from the individual or collective human conscience or soul. Morality is as much an essential aspect of the human arrangement as is speaking or seeing. With perception itself comes evaluation.

The psychotherapeutic relationship is no exception. Psychotherapy is as much a morality play as it is art or science. It is not just about changing behavior, altering cognitions, witnessing trauma, discharging anxiety, resolving emotional conflicts. It is all these things and more. Each system and each practitioner of that approach represents that she or he understands something about how to live a better, freer, more fulfilling life. Ultimately this is what the therapist is selling and what the client is buying. Indeed psychotherapy itself is a process of helping people discover how they should or can live (Real, 1997).

In the beginning, all therapies are applied philosophy, applied epistemology. I would assert that most therapists choose to practice at least partially based on the appeal of grappling on a daily basis with the complex issues raised by the demands of human existence, certainly to help clients do so in better ways. The daily practice of psychotherapy is one route to living the examined life. At least this was so before it became the reimbursed life.

In feminist therapy, each life is more than just examined. There is a commitment to work against injustice, to work for social, as well as personal, change. And feminist therapy is nothing if not judgmental. I mean this, of course, in the broadest and the best sense. I mean the willingness to take a stand when one needs to be taken, to speak out

---

[Haworth co-indexing entry note]: "Beyond the Rule Book." Kaschak, Ellyn. Co-published simultaneously in *Women & Therapy* (The Haworth Press, Inc.) Vol. 22, No. 2, 1999, pp. 1-5; and: *Beyond the Rule Book: Moral Issues and Dilemmas in the Practice of Psychotherapy* (eds: Ellyn Kaschak, and Marcia Hill) The Haworth Press, Inc., 1999, pp. 1-5. Single or multiple copies of this article are available for a fee from The Haworth Document Delivery Service [1-800-342-9678, 9:00 a.m. - 5:00 p.m. (EST). E-mail address: getinfo@haworthpressinc.com].

against oppression, to insist that justice be part of mental health and to make a judgment where a judgment must be made. These are all moral positions.

Long before post-modernism made the idea of moral relativism intellectually popular and palatable, feminists were bold enough to risk being unpopular. And we still are. Although feminism stands firmly for diversity of perspective and experience, it does not join with the post-modern perspective that there is nothing beyond multiple perspectives, with the narrative that there are just equally-valued narratives. Of course there is each person's perspective, each person's truth. And then there is, at least, the material truth. Events actually occur, although they are also interpreted and evaluated. Feminism insists that there is something beyond a marketplace of moralities for the discerning consumer.

These are potentially dangerous ideas. If we openly acknowledge the moral aspect of psychotherapy, then whose morality do we follow? Who decides this and how? Yet there is a greater danger in not acknowledging what exists, a danger that feminism recognizes all too readily. Not acknowledging that psychotherapy is a moral enterprise is akin to not acknowledging that it is also a political act. It is never just one thing, but what it is must not be denied, must not be kept invisible.

There are clear ways in which we can proceed so that the moral path does not turn into a slippery slope beneath our feet. First, theorists and practitioners should not conspire to keep invisible the moral aspects of the enterprise in which we are all engaged, should not pretend that it is not infused with moral issues. The often heard response that the therapist is simply facilitating the client's choices, even if it were possible, is itself a moral position with serious implications.

Secondly I would propose that moral education be part of the training and education of all therapists. By this, I do not mean learning the ethical code, which has become standard practice in the last twenty years. I mean thinking deeply about the moral base of the ethical code; thinking in complex ways about how one comes to develop moral and ethical positions; and understanding in a conscious way that knowing how to ask moral questions and think about, even debate about, the answers is part of any practice that affects and hopes to change people's lives.

Therapists must not just learn to ask what is ethical, but must learn how to decide and how to continue to question even after deciding.

For therapists deciding is a process, not an endpoint. This process can be taught. We can use our base in research to help answer these questions. We can also offer explicit training in philosophy and epistemology. And we must because we are already making moral decisions in every therapeutic relationship whether we emphasize taking personal responsibility for oneself, for others, to others, expressing feelings openly, fulfilling and becoming aware of one's own needs. In addition to their other aspects, these are all moral positions.

The questions need to be both large and small, both inside and outside the frame of the therapeutic hour. Outside: What is a moral life? What is the role of psychotherapy in a moral society? In a not so moral society? In helping to bring about a moral society? Inside: What are the moral implications of encouraging someone to get in touch with and act on her own needs rather than those of the larger group? Of seeing clients individually out of their social contexts and away from any perspectives other than their own on a particular problem? If a client is abusive or worse in his or her relationships, do feminist therapists have any obligation to the partner or other person(s) in these relationships other than those specifically legislated? When and how should the therapist emphasize the client's responsibility to others before or along with the client's responsibility to self? Does individual therapy reinforce narcissism–getting in touch with one's own needs before or instead of those of others? Does it reflect or reinforce American individualistic values such as individual growth, raising self-esteem or asserting individual rights? What about telling the truth in therapy? Is lying ever justified? On the part of the therapist? The client? These are all rooted in the largest questions about being a human being, about living a conscious and moral life.

Third, there must be ongoing self-examination, discussion and debate about morality among professionals and with clients when appropriate. Yet there is currently little discussion of the topic. I do not mean the rule book or the ethical codes of the professional associations, which are, of course, based in the shared and agreed upon morality of the profession as it is currently practiced. The ethical code can permit us to believe that we need not think deeply and carefully about the larger questions, about the uncodified decisions and especially about those interventions that do not even appear to the therapist to be moral ones.

Any ethical code derives from particular moral beliefs. Yet a code is never enough. There are all the situations where the code must be applied and interpreted, the many to which it does not speak, where the practitioner must make her own decision. Each article in this collection in its own way makes visible the decision-making process when it doesn't easily fit into the anticipated circumstances of the codes.

This collection of articles is meant to serve as a contribution to opening a dialogue among us about the moral aspects of psychotherapy by considering specifically the role of morality in therapeutic practice. The ethical code of the Feminist Therapy Institute (1990) explicitly acknowledges its base in feminist morality and many of the authors in this volume, including Sally Keller, Lynne Carroll, Paula Gilroy and Jennifer Murra and Cynthia Bruns and Teresa Lesko explicitly refer to that moral base in their discussions. Others, including Sharla Kibel, Lynda Warwick, Alexandra Bloom and Kayla Weiner, seek guidance from a perhaps more controversial, less secular and more ancient source, the Hebrew or Christian Bibles.

The feminist principle of empowerment is a central one to most of the authors. Several of them ask how to empower individuals in the context of agencies or systems that disempower them. Sharla Kibel considers the empowerment of adolescents and children in an agency context, while Sally Keller focuses on the moral, ethical and therapeutic concerns in a child custody dispute. Lynda Warwick also grapples with the divided loyalties of a feminist therapist to agency and client, while Cynthia Bruns and Teresa Lesko discuss their work with women in prisons. They make explicit what is implied in the other two, a feminist moral obligation to subvert disempowering systems from within.

Several of the authors focus on particular issues or populations. Kayla Weiner is particularly concerned with how to incorporate a sense of morality into therapeutic decisions, while Rhoda Olkin considers specific moral issues in working with clients with disabilities. Gayle Pitman discusses the morality of feminist naming with a particular focus on lesbian-feminist "rules" about sexuality and appearance. Lynne Carroll, Paula Gilroy and Jennifer Murra base their discussion of the moral imperative of self-care for therapists on their survey results.

As Alexandra Bloom so aptly notes, therapy done without a moral stance is, by definition, demoralizing to the therapist and the client. In this so-called post-feminist, post-modern era, morality often appears to be exhausted. Yet the truth is that neither morality nor we feminists are obsolete. There is more than enough for us to do to counter the demoralizing effects on our clients and ourselves of many aspects of the agencies in which we practice, the funding on which we depend and the problems of ordinary and not-so-ordinary life that must be faced every day. And there are new generations of feminist therapists to join us in developing the theory and practice to do so. We are still asking the important questions, still making the invisible visible and still have the courage to be unpopular.

Ellyn Kaschak

REFERENCES

Feminist Therapy Institute, Inc. (1990). Feminist Therapy Institute Code of Ethics. In H. Lerman & N. Porter (Eds.), *Feminist ethics in psychotherapy* (pp. 37-40). New York: Springer Publishing Company.

Real, Terrence (1997). *I don't want to talk about it: Overcoming the secret legacy of male depression.* New York: Scribner.

The Ostrich Raises Its Head: "Knowing" and Moral Accountability in the Practice of Psychotherapy

Alexandra Bloom

SUMMARY. What is "knowing" in psychotherapy? What impact does it have on patients and therapists? Does knowing have moral relevance? This paper explores these questions through traditional, feminist, and psychoanalytic critiques of epistemology. Countertransference issues are addressed, including a discussion of therapists' resistances to knowing about their patients' realities. The author proposes that when therapists can truly "know" their patients, and patients are able to know themselves, moral responsiveness and accountability ensue. *[Article copies available for a fee from The Haworth Document Delivery Service: 1-800-342-9678. E-mail address: getinfo@haworthpressinc.com]*

KEYWORDS. Knowing, epistemology, psychoanalysis, morality, feminism

When I was a teenager, my mother and sister chided me for not watching the news. My refusal to give even a passing glance to the

---

Alexandra Bloom is currently a doctoral candidate at the Derner Institute for Advanced Psychological Studies, Adelphi University.

The author would like to thank Mary Solberg, whose work is the inspiration for this paper, and who has been a dear friend and role model for both intellectual and emotional knowing. She also thanks Tana Bloom, whose moral vision helped shape this paper.

Address correspondence to: Alexandra Bloom, MA, The Derner Institute, Adelphi University, Garden City, NY 11530. (E-mail: blooma@panther.adelphi.edu).

[Haworth co-indexing entry note]: "The Ostrich Raises Its Head: 'Knowing' and Moral Accountability in the Practice of Psychotherapy." Bloom, Alexandra. Co-published simultaneously in *Women & Therapy* (The Haworth Press, Inc.) Vol. 22, No. 2, 1999, pp. 7-20; and: *Beyond the Rule Book: Moral Issues and Dilemmas in the Practice of Psychotherapy* (eds: Ellyn Kaschak, and Marcia Hill) The Haworth Press, Inc., 1999, pp. 7-20. Single or multiple copies of this article are available for a fee from The Haworth Document Delivery Service [1-800-342-9678, 9:00 a.m. - 5:00 p.m. (EST). E-mail address: getinfo@haworthpress inc.com].

© 1999 by The Haworth Press, Inc. All rights reserved.

newspaper invited their epistemological critique: You're like an ostrich, with your head in the sand. My eyes and ears fully submerged, I refused to know about the violence and destruction of the world. Now, as an adult and a developing therapist, my capacity to know and to resist denial has gradually evolved; reading the newspaper every day is just one manifestation of my facing up to the painful reality we live in, both externally and, often, internally. I believe my ongoing struggle points to a dilemma faced by all therapists: How do we "know" about another's suffering, without either denying it or falling into despair? If and when we do come to terms with what we know, how does this transform us and the work we do? Are we morally implicated in our patients' lives, both through how and what we know about ourselves and them? What role does morality play in an individual's emotional growth?

MODELS OF EPISTEMOLOGY

Before these questions can be explored, the word "knowing" must be examined, for it is an enormously complicated and controversial term. Within the field of psychotherapy, how knowing occurs has been widely disputed. How does a therapist come to know a patient? What sources of information generate "real" knowledge? Is it important to know what is real in an historical sense, or can we be content to arrive at a narrative which seems useful to the patient? What gives the therapist the authority to know? To address these questions, I will examine changing models of epistemology within psychoanalytic theory. I will also show how feminist and postmodernist theories have provided vital critiques of both psychoanalysis and traditional epistemology, spurring transformations and growth in both domains.

Freud's psychoanalytic theory radically called into question traditional ideas about what we can know about ourselves and other people. Enlightenment philosophers' faith in the powers of reason and empiricists' belief in the reliability of sense perception and observation relied on a conception of mind which was unimpinged upon by unconscious needs and desires; the Freudian model of mind, in contrast, is constituted through a dialectic of inner and outer experiences, which are simultaneously psychic, somatic, object related, cultural, and historical (Flax, 1990). In spite of this major revision of the nature of subjectivity, however, Freudian epistemology remained essentially positivistic; the inherent obscurities involved in a person's quest for self-understanding were not generalized to the practice of scientific information-gathering. According to Freud, "the intellect and the mind are objects for scientific research in exactly the same way as any non-human things" (1933, p. 197). Although he recognized that reality was not transparent, nevertheless he believed the purpose of science was:

> to arrive at correspondence with reality–that is to say, with what exists outside us and independently of us and, as experience has taught us, is decisive for the fulfillment or disappointment of our wishes. This correspondence with the external world we call "truth." (p. 211)

Freud presciently spoke to the relativistic position that has been articulated by postmodernist philosophers:

> According to the anarchist theory there is no such thing as truth, no assured knowledge of the external world. What we give out as being scientific truth is only the product of our own needs as they are bound to find utterance under changing external conditions: once again, they are illusion. Fundamentally, we find only what we need and see only what we want to see. We have no other possibility. Since the criterion of truth–correspondence with the external world–is absent, it is entirely a matter of indifference what opinions we adopt. All of them are equally true and equally false. And no one has a right to accuse anyone else of error. (p. 217)

Wanting to safeguard psychoanalysis from charges of pseudoscience, Freud attempted to provide an objective basis for his new methods. He believed rigorous application of psychoanalytic technique could yield truths about patients' emotional worlds. In order to keep the analytic situation uncontaminated by the influence of the therapist's person, Freud recommended abstinence. In this way, analysts would be prevented from projecting their own pathology on their patients. Freud recognized, however, that the analyst's reaction to the patient needed to be managed in some way beyond mere abstinence. Introducing the term "countertransference" in 1910, he wrote:

> We have become aware of the "counter-transference," which arises in the physician as a result of the patient's influence on his unconscious feelings, and we are almost inclined to insist that he shall recognize his counter-transference in himself and overcome it. (p. 144)

Tansey and Burke (1989) point out the ambiguity of Freud's recommendation. Did he mean that countertransference is only an impediment, arising from the analyst's unresolved conflicts? Or can the countertransference response be mutually created? Until recently, the former conceptualization has prevailed in psychoanalytic thinking. This stance reflects the traditional ideas about science that Freud promulgated: The subject (scientist) examines the object (patient) in a manner which does not significantly implicate the personality of the scientist.

FEMINIST CRITIQUES OF TRADITIONAL EPISTEMOLOGY

Many feminist theorists have argued that this subject/object dichotomy is untenable, and reflects a particular type of male bias. Keller (1985) contends that the terms of scientific exploration are implicitly gendered. Men are the observers, women the territory to be explored and deciphered. Further, she suggests that men's position as "objective observers" is congruent with a particular cultural myth of rugged, male individuality:

> My argument is not simply that the dream of a completely objective science is in principle unrealizable, but that it contains precisely what it rejects: the vivid traces of a reflected self image. The objectivist illusion reflects back an image of self as autonomous and objectified: an image of individuals unto themselves, severed from the outside world of other objects (animate as well as inanimate) and simultaneously from their own subjectivity. (p. 70)

This distance is inherent in the notion of the "neutral" analytic observer, and limits the therapist from full engagement with the affective material generated both by the patient and between the therapeutic dyad. As Keller writes of traditional scientific epistemology, "the modes of intercourse are defined so as to ensure emotional and physical inviolability for the subject" (p. 79). Chodorow's (1978) developmental theory, elaborating the consequences of the fact that most children's primary affective ties are to women, suggests why a blurring of boundaries between subject and object would be associated with the feminine.

Other feminists critiquing the construction of knowledge in psychology have noted that women have been excluded as both subjects and observers, and have documented the biasing effects this has had on psychological science (Maccoby and Jacklin, 1974; Miller, 1976; Squire, 1989; Weisstein, 1973). Gilligan's (1982) re-examination of Kohlberg's stages of moral development, for example, suggests that women use different criteria than men when making moral decisions, and that this divergence has to do with the different culturally determined roles they play. In general, these feminist assessments have highlighted the extent to which science is not neutral, but is shaped by the values and interests of its creators. This position has also been fruitfully explored by postmodernist philosophers, who have demonstrated the subtle ways in which cultural ideology masks itself as "truth" or "science" (see, for example, Derrida, 1978; Foucault, 1965; Haraway, 1989).

CONTEMPORARY PSYCHOANALYTIC EPISTEMOLOGY

Psychoanalytic thought has shifted in parallel with feminist and postmodernist questionings of the status of "knowing." For example, analysts now question whether the exploration of the patient's psyche and past yields narrative or historical truth (Spence, 1982). If transference involves an attribution of authority to the knowledge of the analyst, how can the analyst's interpretations avoid biasing the patient's construction of reality? From where do the analyst's interpretations spring–out of a genuine understanding of the patient's internal world, from a projection of the analyst's internal world, or some mesh of the two? The ambiguities brought to light by feminist and postmodern critiques of traditional scientific "objectivity" and epistemology show that there is no place to stand of innocence or neutrality; rather, any time we try to know we are infusing ourselves into our "object" of inquiry. As therapists, we become implicated both by our use of theory and by our idiosyncratic countertransference reactions.

Hoffman (1996) argues that this involvement with patients nullifies the possibility of both analytic and moral neutrality. In the same way that analysts have shied away from the full implications of their countertransference reactions, they have defensively retreated from knowing the full weight of their moral involvement with patients. The ideal analytic stance runs thus: analysts help their patients gain a richer understanding of their unconscious motivations, thereby allowing them greater freedom in their choices. Ultimately, however, the patient makes choices and life decisions alone. Hoffman, questioning whether the analyst can truly escape influencing patients' life decisions, writes:

> I think that the idea of analysis as sanctuary, taken too literally, denies both the extent of our authority and the extent of our intimate involvement with our patients as they risk doing or not doing one thing or another both inside and outside the analytic situation. In trying so hard to stay out of it we can really be "out of it." Opportune moments for action come and go. They do not necessarily recur and they certainly do not last forever. The analyst is right there in the patient's life as those moments pass by. (p. 107)

According to Hoffman, because the analyst is involved in both the construction and the discovery of the patient's emotional reality, there is no way to limit her involvement to being merely a facilitator of the patient's self awareness. Inevitably, the analyst will selectively attend to some of the patient's material, will attune to or miss different emotional states, will question or leave unchallenged certain of the patient's assumptions. These selectively attended to elements of the patient's experience will emerge from whatever particular transference-countertransference chemistry is created in the therapeutic dyad. Whatever that may be, the analyst's use of herself as an instrument has, as it must, transformative effects on the therapeutic work. As Hoffman writes, "there is an ongoing tension and oscillation between the conscious and unconscious building up of 'realities' in one sphere or another, and reflection upon how, why, and at what cost these particular constructions arose and became more or less calcified" (p. 113). Given that psychic reality is co-constructed, it is incumbent upon the therapist to be cognizant and wise in the wielding of her influence.

KNOWING AND MORAL ACCOUNTABILITY

Emerging from the sanctuary of analytic neutrality, I turn once again to the moral significance of knowing, which I believe plays a crucial role in the dynamics of therapy. I will rely on Solberg's (1997) work to introduce the relevant issues:

> Much that people know matters very little to them. That is to say, people know a great many things that do not make any discernible difference in their day-to-day lives. . . . In most cases, of course, what people know has instrumental significance for what they do. Knowing something makes it possible to do something, or to avoid or stop doing something. Scattered across a continuum, people are more or less able, well- or ill-positioned, to make use of all kinds of things they know. When people either fail to act or act inappropriately, others may well associate what they did or did not do with what they knew or did not know (including "know how to do") in this instrumental sense. (p. 2)

Once people come to know something, this knowing may compel them to behave differently than if they had not known. Solberg contends that knowing invites a moral response, an integration of what has been learned beyond mere formal information. Translated into the language of psychotherapy, knowing, or awareness, allows people to change how they live their lives. The morality that ensues from this, I believe, takes the form of treating others well. To my way of thinking, a hallmark of emotional health is following the "golden rule" of morality: Do unto others as you would have them do unto you. In this vision, to become healthier emotionally is to become simultaneously more morally responsible.

DEMORALIZATION

People come to therapy because they are *demoralized*–alienated from a sense of meaning, purpose, or cohesion in their lives. Vaclav Havel writes that one " . . . who has no roots in the order of being, no sense of responsibility for anything higher than his or her own personal survival, is a *demoralized* person" (1986/1978, p. 62). Indeed, a person struggling against falling apart feels desperate to insure psychic survival. The cost of this psychic survival often involves a withdrawal into narcissistic or self serving modes of being. The embattled psyche tries to defend itself through grasping tightly what it tenuously holds: some advantage, power differential, or way of "winning" and avoiding loss. Or, in the absence of this fighting spirit, the self simply withdraws and isolates, sealing off potentially damaging contact with the world. Whether exploitative or petrified, the individual is indeed de-moralized–cut off from emotionally meaningful and reciprocal relationships. In this state, one is ill-disposed to treat others in a morally responsible manner.

Psychopathology, it could be argued, always involves a retreat from emotional or material reality. Psychosis, depression, mania, pathological narcissism, and borderline personality functioning all compromise one's ability to treat others with the respect and care they deserve. Whatever form our psychopathology takes, we all wish to avoid loss and pain. To make morally responsible decisions, however, loss and pain often cannot be evaded. Behaving morally or ethically is difficult precisely because we cannot exploit another or a situation to our full advantage. We must concede what could be ours for the well-being of another or for a greater good. For a person who feels psychically impoverished and depleted, this is nearly impossible. Through therapy, however, this depletion can be addressed. The therapist's task is to model and facilitate emotional maturity, which in turn leads to improved relationships. When the therapist is consistent, straightforward, non-retaliating, and unexploitable, she is modeling the golden rule, and laying the groundwork for a patient's incorporation of these qualities. Both patient and therapist must also work to accept and live in reality, resisting the urge to retreat defensively.

CLINICAL IMPLICATIONS

What does all this mean for the practice of therapy? I do not believe that therapists should moralize, criticize, or thrust upon their patients ill-timed confrontations; nor am I suggesting that they should discourage their patients from expressing "non-realistic" feelings or fantasies. Rather, I believe that therapists should provide an atmosphere of safety so that patients can experience and reveal what they have disowned, and that they should use their comments and interpretations to facilitate this process. I believe that an honest confrontation with who one is, warts and all, fertilizes the ground from which more reciprocal relationships can grow. In contrast, when one refuses to know oneself, one's disavowed feelings interfere with good relationships. There are powerful resistances to seeing one's underbelly, of course; we have to give up our omnipotent fantasies, and reveal our vulnerable wounds. The therapist, in turn, to be equal to the task, must be unafraid to see and experience all of the patient, though the patient's revelations may be shrouded in shame. Although the task appears straightforward, I believe there are powerful resistances to therapists' ability to know their patients' psychic realities.

One resistance springs from fear of becoming merged with the patient's disorganized or despairing internal state. This is especially true when working with patients with trauma histories (Davies & Frawley, 1994; Herman, 1992). Those who have suffered multiple losses often have internal worlds filled with unbearable pain, and communicate this pain vividly and unmistakably to therapists by drawing them into reenacting early chaotic relationships (Davies & Frawley, 1994). A corollary to this resistance is the therapist's fear of recognizing similarities to herself in the patient's pathology; therapists often have a vested interest in seeing themselves as healthy, and their patients as sick (Racker, 1968; Searles, 1979). As understandable as these resistances might be, however, their existence underscores the importance of their resolution. Particularly in the case of parental physical or sexual abuse, there is enormous pressure on the survivor not to know her own experience, both in an attempt to preserve an inner psychic equilibrium, and to resist implicating a loved caretaker. I believe this resistance to knowing can hold true even with patients with less potent psychic turmoil; in general, psychological defenses mask painful emotions. Reik, describing the results of psychoanalytic insight, wrote, "This new knowledge confronts us with dangers that we seemed to have mastered long ago, raises thoughts that we had not dared to think, stirs feelings from which we had anxiously guarded ourselves" (1949, p. 504). Confronting and acknowledging these disowned parts of experience or history creates the need to mourn losses. In *Trauma and Recovery*, Herman describes the integrity needed to do therapy effectively and honestly; the therapist must have "the capacity to affirm the value of life in the face of death, to be reconciled with the finite limits of one's own life and the tragic limitations of the human condition and to accept these realities without despair" (1992, p. 154). Herman's moral vision is congruent with Solberg's: Morality lies in honest confrontation and acknowledgement of what is the case, as wrenching as it is. I do not believe this vision depends upon an ability to know with certainty or facts; rather, it depends on knowing with emotional honesty, imperfect and clouded though it may be.

Another major resistance to knowing is in recognizing the extent to which we are implicated in systems which perpetuate injustice. We resist knowing how the parts of our subjectivity which are privileged in this culture, such as being White, heterosexual, or having money, situate our perceptions in ways which blind us to power imbalances. For example, Wasserstrom (1976) describes a situation involving an all White jury and a Black defendant. The case against the defendant was based entirely on the testimony of the police, and an eyewitness and forensic evidence contradicted their account. Nevertheless, the jury spent seven hours deliberating before returning a verdict of an acquittal. Why so long? Wasserstrom attributes the jury's slowness in reaching the correct decision to their difficulty believing the police could deliberately fabricate a story. Nothing in their White, middle class existence suggested that this might be a likely occurrence. Invisible frameworks such as these cloud our perception continually; we resist seeing them because we do not want to recognize our participation in unjust or discriminatory practices. Solberg writes:

> The reality of a 'dominant meaning system' that ignores the experiences of certain groups–in particular the experiences of suffering that are more often and more egregiously the lot of marginalized groups than of privileged ones–has a pervasive effect on the sensibilities and possibilities of even the most conscientious individuals living within the system's ambit. (p. 129)

To counter our conscription into dominant meaning systems, we must try to unmask the invisible frameworks we operate within. To the extent that we have subjectivities which are not privileged in this culture–such as being women, people of color, gay or lesbian, or poor, we must attend to ways in which we come to know the world differently from the margins. This awareness has enormous consequences for how we apprehend the realities of patients who have different configurations of privilege than we do. It is only in grappling with viewpoints which may elude our usual experience that we are able to have a full empathic range.

THE GENESIS OF KNOWING

Finally, I would like to discuss the genesis of "knowing" which I believe best facilitates the kind of awareness I have been discussing. This knowing is not intellectual, nor is it meant to yield veridical truth. As feminist, postmodern, and psychoanalytic critics of traditional science and epistemology have demonstrated, this is not an attainable, or necessarily desirable goal. Contrary to the model of subject "knowing" object, psychoanalytic object relational theories stress an interaction which is reciprocally generated and constructed. The therapist's countertransference reaction, seen in the past as contaminating or disrupting the understanding of analytic material, is now seen as organizing and enriching it. This understanding, however, must be tempered with the therapist's self understanding; countertransference data cannot be taken as the new supplier of veridical truth. The knowing I believe is the key to full engagement with the patient is akin to what Bruner (1986) called "perfinking": the ability to perceive, feel, and think at the same time. The roots of this apprehension of ourselves and others are to be found in earliest childhood development. Stern (1985) has written of how children come to know themselves and others through the emotional mediation of a good parent:

> It is clear that interpersonal communication, as created by attunement, will play an important role in the infant's coming to recognize that internal feeling states are forms of human experience that are shareable with other humans. The converse is also true: feeling states that are never attuned to will be experienced only alone, isolated from the interpersonal context of shareable experience. What is at stake is nothing less than the shape of and extent of the shareable inner universe. (pp. 151-152)

Stern's theory and research highlights the extent to which interactions between child and caretaker are constitutive of the child's experienced emotions. The more attuned the parent is to the child, the more likely it is that the child will have access to a full range of emotion. If the parent does not attune to, or does not acknowledge, certain affective states, these affective states are likely to be disallowed and not available to be experienced directly. Similarly, the goal of therapy is to facilitate access to disallowed emotional experiences. To facilitate this awareness, the therapist must be engaged in an ongoing struggle with resistances to knowing about these experiences, both in herself and in her patients. It is through the therapist's willingness and capacity to be aware that a genuine human link is forged within the therapeutic dyad. Bion (1962) conceptualized thinking as the emotional experience of trying to know oneself or someone else. He argued that a formidable therapeutic resistance arises when patients attack a meaningful understanding of their experience. Rather than understanding their experience, he believed, people often strip it of its import in order to avoid anxious emotional states, thus leaving it lifeless and dead. Despite this resistance, however, patients also do "anxiety ridden research" into their therapists' minds–searching for the existence of a capacity to "think, notice, remember, tell the difference between truth and lies, and emotionally understand–as opposed to verbally, mechanically, or from books" (O'Shaughnessy, 1981, p. 187). This capacity, I believe, is the key to a genuine therapeutic awareness which resists denial. It makes it possible for the therapist to treat the patient with the greatest possible sensitivity, creating a morally accountable therapy.

Though I have drawn upon more contemporary sources in building my argument, these ideas are not new. In 1949, Reik wrote:

> Courage seems to me one of the finest virtues, for it excludes many faults, like lying, hypocrisy, and insincerity. In many cases it is not lack of courage and acumen, *but lack of moral courage that prevents us from comprehending the hidden meaning of unconscious processes.* . . . We see more and more clearly that the conditions of psychological comprehension are less intellectual than characterological. In order to bring the hidden truth of the unconscious to the light of day, we need not only science but also conscience. (p. 500)

What is crucial to doing the work of therapy effectively and courageously is not intellect, but a particular type of characterological strength, that involves the fullest possible integration of one's own emotional experience, as well as receptivity to another's. I believe that Reik's words are true not only for the resistance of coming to terms with unconscious material, but also with resistance to the full emotional impact of consciously presented material. The moral imperative here is to use one's self fully–without the therapist's full and committed presence, the therapy may be sterile and mired in maintaining defenses and denial. Reik continued:

> It is correct to say that the analyst's most significant knowledge must be experienced by himself. But it is even more correct and approaches nearer to what is essential to declare openly that these psychological experiences are of such a nature that they must be suffered. . . . Perhaps the subjective capacity to suffer or, better, the capacity to accept and assimilate painful knowledge, is one of the most important prognostic marks of analytic study. . . . And this capacity is assuredly not one that can be learned. Suffering, too, is a gift; it is a grace. (pp. 504-505)

Thus therapists are entrusted with an enormously stimulating and daunting task, for in "accepting and assimilating painful knowledge" we are pushed to confront our own denials and obfuscations of internal and external reality, and are spurred to grow through new emotional integrations. In this process, we continually struggle against not-knowing in order to take up and greet our moral charge, just as the ostrich shakes the sand from its head and looks out upon the day.

REFERENCES

Bion, W. (1962). *Learning from experience*. London: Heinemann.
Bruner, J.S. (1986). *Actual minds, possible worlds*. Cambridge, MA: Harvard Univ. Press.
Chodorow, N. (1978). *The reproduction of mothering: Psychoanalysis and the sociology of gender*. Berkeley: University of California Press.
Davies, J.M. & Frawley, M.G. (1994). *Treating the adult survivor of childhood sexual abuse*. New York: Basic Books.
Derrida, J. (1978). *Writing and difference*. (A. Bass, Trans.). Chicago: University of Chicago Press.
Flax, J. (1990). *Thinking fragments: Psychoanalysis, feminism, and postmodernism in the contemporary west*. Berkeley, CA: University of California Press.
Foucault, M. (1965). *Madness and civilization*. New York: Vintage.
Freud, S. (1910). The future prospects of psychoanalytic therapy. *Standard Edition, 11*, 141-151. London: Hogarth Press, 1953.
Freud, S. (1933). The question of a weltanschauung. *New introductory lectures on psycho-analysis*. New York: W.W. Norton.
Gilligan, C. (1982). *In a different voice*. Cambridge, MA: Harvard University Press.

Haraway, D. (1989). *Primate visions: Gender, race, and nature in the world of modern science.* New York: Routledge.
Havel, V. (1986). The power of the powerless. In J. Vladislav (Ed.) *Living in truth.* Boston: Faber and Faber. (Original essay published 1978).
Herman, J.L. (1992). *Trauma and recovery.* New York: Basic Books.
Hoffman, I.Z. (1996). The intimate and ironic authority of the psychoanalyst's presence. *Psychoanalytic Quarterly, 65,* (1) 102-136.
Keller, E.F. (1985). *Reflections on gender and science.* New Haven, CT: Yale University Press.
Maccoby, E. & Jacklin, C. (1974). *The psychology of sex differences.* Stanford, CA: Stanford University Press.
Miller, J.B. (1976). *Toward a new psychology of women.* Boston, MA: Beacon Press.
O'Shaughnessy, E. (1981). W.R. Bion's theory of thinking and new techniques in child analysis. *Journal of Child Psychotherapy, 7,* (2), 181-189.
Racker, H. (1968). *Transference and countertransference.* New York: International Universities Press.
Reik, T. (1949). *Listening with the third ear.* New York: Farrar, Straus and Company.
Searles, H. (1979). The dedicated physician. In *Countertransference.* New York: International Universities Press.
Solberg, M.M. (1997). *Compelling knowledge: A feminist proposal for an epistemology of the cross.* Albany, NY: State University of New York Press.
Spence, D.P. (1982). *Narrative truth and historical truth: Meaning and interpretation in psychoanalysis.* New York: W.W. Norton.
Squire, C. (1989). *Significant differences: Feminism in psychology.* New York: Routledge.
Stern, D. (1985). *The interpersonal world of the human infant.* New York: Basic Books.
Tansey, M.J. & Burke, W.F. (1989). *Understanding countertransference.* New Jersey: The Analytic Press.
Wasserstrom, R. (1976). The university and the case for preferential treatment. *American Philosophical Quarterly 13,* (2), 165-170.
Weisstein, N. (1973). Kind, kuche, kirche as scientific law: Psychology constructs the female. In P. Brown (Ed.) *Radical Psychology.* New York: Harper Colophon.

The Politics of Naming and the Development of Morality: Implications for Feminist Therapists

Gayle E. Pitman

SUMMARY. Feminists have challenged traditional uses of naming and have reclaimed naming as a tool of empowerment rather than of oppression. Yet feminist naming often reverts into the paradigm of dominant culture, leading to further domination and social control through the creation of norms, rules, and moral absolutes. By focusing specifically on lesbian-feminism and deconstructing the lesbian-feminist "rules" of sexuality and physical appearance, this article explores the dualistic nature of feminist naming and morality and how they inadvertently mimic the moral paradigm of dominant culture. This article closes with a discussion of alternative models of feminist naming and moral frameworks. *[Article copies available for a fee from The Haworth Document Delivery Service: 1-800-342-9678. E-mail address: getinfo@haworthpressinc.com]*

Gayle E. Pitman is a doctoral candidate at the California School of Professional Psychology-Alameda. Her dissertation research was on body dissatisfaction and internalized homophobia in lesbians, and her other interests include body image and eating disorders in lesbians, the impact of cultural oppression on mental health, and feminist ethics. She is currently completing her predoctoral internship at the University of California at Santa Cruz, Counseling and Psychological Services.

The author would like to thank Shannon Mullally, Kristen Valus, Diana E. H. Russell, Marcia Hill, and Ellyn Kaschak for their helpful suggestions and editorial comments.

Address correspondence to: Gayle E. Pitman, California School of Professional Psychology-Alameda, 1005 Atlantic Avenue, Alameda, CA 94501.

[Haworth co-indexing entry note]: "The Politics of Naming and the Development of Morality: Implications for Feminist Therapists." Pitman, Gayle E. Co-published simultaneously in *Women & Therapy* (The Haworth Press, Inc.) Vol. 22, No. 2, 1999, pp. 21-38; and: *Beyond the Rule Book: Moral Issues and Dilemmas in the Practice of Psychotherapy* (eds: Ellyn Kaschak, and Marcia Hill) The Haworth Press, Inc., 1999, pp. 21-38. Single or multiple copies of this article are available for a fee from The Haworth Document Delivery Service [1-800-342-9678, 9:00 a.m. - 5:00 p.m. (EST). E-mail address: getinfo@haworthpressinc.com].

© 1999 by The Haworth Press, Inc. All rights reserved.

KEYWORDS. Feminism, ethics, morality, lesbians, feminist therapy

Feminism has clearly made a significant impact on the lives of women in Western culture. By naming "the problem that has no name" (Friedan, 1963), feminists sparked a revolution that led to enormous changes in women's lives. Within the rubric of liberal feminism, women began to challenge gender inequities and fight for equal rights and opportunities. Radical feminism enabled women to challenge male-dominated institutions, to move beyond the control of men, and to create a woman-centered environment, which empowered lesbians to come out and to assert their personal and political freedom. And cultural feminism set the stage for challenging other forms of oppression, including racism, classism, and homophobia. Clearly, naming various oppressions and adopting a feminist belief system has had far-reaching implications for women.

Naming diminishes the power an idea or concept has over us, the power of that which is unconscious, by bringing it to consciousness and allowing us to look it in the eye. The naming of oppression and misogyny by feminists has enabled women to diminish its power, fight against sexism and homophobia, and create a community offering identity, validation, and empowerment. Yet, paradoxically, naming can itself become the site of oppression by creating norms, moral frameworks and standards of correctness, and rules which govern the actions of the oppressed–a very powerful act which can ultimately undermine an individual's identity, which excludes those who don't fit the normative standards, and which functions as a means of social control. Within the lesbian-feminist community, for example, naming heterosexist and misogynist oppression has led to the creation of lesbian-feminist group norms, values, rules, and moral standards–standards which lead to exclusionary practices within the community and which mimic the oppressive moral framework and standards of correctness in dominant culture. Thus, lesbians who stray from the rigid expectations of the lesbian-feminist community and who contradict the conventional wisdom of what a "good feminist" or a "real lesbian" should be will ultimately be excluded and rejected, leading to feelings of shame, guilt, and isolation, fostering divisiveness and undermining the goals of the feminist movement.

In this article, I explore issues surrounding the politics of naming and address how naming operates specifically within the lesbian-feminist community. While naming the existence of oppression is a vitally important step in eliminating it, feminist naming has also led to the creation of a lesbian-feminist community with morals, rules, and values–not unlike other organizations, communities, and institutions which govern and police the actions of its members–replacing "compulsory heterosexuality" (Rich, 1980) with compulsory radical lesbian-feminism and creating its own version of social control. By deconstructing the "rules" around sexual practices and physical appearance within the lesbian-feminist community, I will illustrate how feminist morality has evolved into a means of social control, mimicking the moral paradigm of dominant culture and resulting in the undermining of feminist goals. I will close by addressing how leaving this dissonance unnamed ultimately perpetuates oppression and subordination, and illustrate how, paradoxically, the ongoing process of challenging and redefining feminist values, morals, and ethics can be a powerful means of combating institutionalized sexism and homophobia.

THE POLITICS OF NAMING: TRADITIONAL VS. FEMINIST

Naming is an act which takes place within the context of a society which values hierarchy, individual responsibility, independence and autonomy, and personal control. Moreover, naming often reflects and reinforces the moral framework of society. Within dominant culture, morality is a system of ideas dictating what is right or wrong, the goal of which is not to promote virtuosity or the overall well-being of society, but for those in power to maintain their dominant position. For example, the "family values" of the 1980s was an attempt to undermine the feminist movement under the rubric of "morality"; marriage, mothering, homemaking, and bearing children were constructed as "moral" choices for women, while lesbianism, having children outside the context of heterosexual marriage, and working outside the home (particularly mothers), even out of necessity, were all viewed as "immoral." For members of oppressed groups, who, due to economic and institutional restrictions, are more likely to fall into the latter group of behaviors, these acts of naming moral and immoral behaviors creates an even stronger power differential and reinforces the control the dominant group has over oppressed groups.

The most common and institutionally sanctioned example of naming within the field of psychology is diagnosis. Within the traditional mental health system, diagnosis has clearly been abused and used to depoliticize and obscure political issues, to punish individuals with a pathologizing label, and to further disempower oppressed groups by labeling their difficulties as the fault of the individual rather than as the result of larger cultural forces. Members of oppressed groups are typically given diagnoses which decontextualize their experiences, contribute to further discrimination and oppression, and locate the "disorder" within the individual rather than within culture.

Examples of the abuses of psychological diagnosis abound. For instance:

- The diagnostic nomenclature of the DSM-II (1973) demonstrated the presumption that homosexuality was the result of a mental disturbance, a developmental arrest, or a perversion, rather than a normal aspect of one's identity. While homosexuality has long since been removed from the DSM, it was replaced with the diagnosis of ego-dystonic homosexuality and was not removed until 1988, and it remains a diagnosis within the International Classification of Diseases (ICD) classification system.
- Transgendered individuals are commonly given the diagnosis of "Gender Identity Disorder," which labels their identity as "pathological" while reinforcing the sex and gender norms of dominant society. Moreover, transsexuals must be diagnosed with this "mental disorder" before they can undergo sex reassignment surgery, perpetuating and reinforcing the view that transsexualism is a psychological disturbance.
- As stipulated by the DSM-IV (1994), a woman's "age, sexual experience, and the adequacy of sexual stimulation she receives" (p. 506) are the primary criteria for making a diagnosis of "Female Orgasmic Disorder." These criteria, which are decontextualized and largely behavioristic, are more applicable to male sexuality, and appear to be based on a masculinist paradigm, fail to reflect and address gender-specific factors contributing to orgasmic difficulties, such as intimacy issues within relationships, a history of sexual trauma, and the pervasive sexual objectification women experience from an early age (M. Hill, personal communication, August 26, 1998; Tiefer, 1988). Furthermore, the statement that this condition is usually "lifelong" (p. 505) in-

creases the probability that a woman will be pathologized with this terminal diagnosis.

These are but a few examples of the abusive power of naming and diagnosing. What is of critical importance in analyzing the abuses of diagnosis is that in each of these cases, the diagnosis represents a breach of the morals and standards of dominant society. Gays and lesbians are breaking the rule of compulsory heterosexuality; transsexuals are breaking the rule of the biological and essential nature of gender; and women whose orgasms are not just a matter of "adequate sexual stimulation" are breaking the rules of sexual pleasure as defined from a masculinist perspective. By giving these diagnoses within this context, psychologists are actually containing the threat to the dominant power structure through the imposition of control.

Because of the abuses that result from traditional ways of naming, because naming has commonly been used to uphold and reinforce the power differentials in patriarchal society, and because naming within the moral framework of patriarchy has resulted in countless injustices against oppressed groups, feminist therapists have challenged traditional uses of naming within the field of mainstream psychology. Yet while the concept of "feminist naming" may seemingly be a contradiction, given the power of naming, its relation to and subsequent creation of normative and moral standards, and the strong potential for the abuse of this power, it is important to consider the powerful impact naming has on effecting social change, particularly when the act of naming is done with a clear understanding of its power. Recognizing and naming injustices is often the first step toward change and is a necessary precursor to social movements. When an experience, phenomenon, or idea is named, particularly the experiences of oppressed groups, the very act of naming gives that experience legitimacy and validation, whereas in its unnamed state it is much easier to ignore, dismiss, or deny that experience.

For example, a number of studies indicated a strong correlation between Axis II diagnoses, particularly borderline personality disorder, and histories of childhood sexual abuse in women (Laporte and Guttman, 1996; Weaver and Clum, 1993). Feminist therapists took this finding a step further and argued that, instead of attributing women's distress to longstanding, pathological personality traits, focusing on the abuse issues would be much more useful and empowering to the client, for it provides a direction for treatment, it conveys that the client's problems are treatable and not permanent, and moves away from blaming the victim to placing her distress within a social and environmental context (Porter, n.d.). From there, feminist therapists called for the creation of less stigmatizing and pathologizing diagnostic categories, such as complex PTSD (Herman, 1992) and Abuse Disorder (Zetlin, 1990), which would reduce further stigmatization and more accurately reflect the experiences of the client. With the application of a feminist value system and a clear understanding of the power and political implications of diagnosis, naming the effects of childhood abuse was a powerful tool used by feminist therapists to validate women's experience, acknowledge the impact of the cultural environment, and challenge mainstream diagnostic paradigms.

Undoubtedly, naming and giving voice to an injustice is a vital step in developing an awareness of its negative impact. Naming can empower the oppressed by norming and validating their experience, and it can lead to positive social and institutional changes. With respect to the feminist movement, working towards eliminating oppression and transforming societal institutions would be impossible without naming and acknowledging the presence of sexism, racism, classism, and homophobia in our culture. Yet while naming our experience can be validating and empowering, feminist naming also has the power to create further oppression, particularly when it is done blindly and without an understanding of the implications of naming a particular phenomenon. While feminist naming is typically done in the service of challenging the norms of dominant culture, like traditional naming it often leads to the creation of a new set of norms which can potentially evolve into moral judgments and standards of correctness, ultimately leading to coercion rather than empowerment (Ballou, 1995; Hoagland, 1988). Whereas the violation of patriarchal standards of correctness by feminists may be seen as positive (for example, lesbian-feminists who react against dominant culture's standard of compulsory heterosexuality are lauded and embraced by other members of the lesbian-feminist community), within the lesbian-feminist community, violating the norms of the community and challenging lesbian-feminist "morals" can result in serious and far-reaching consequences, not unlike the consequences of challenging the norms and morals of patriarchy. As an illustration of these repercussions, in the next section I will focus specifically on lesbian-feminism and discuss how the dialectics of naming ultimately thwarted lesbian-feminist goals.

NAMING AND THE DEVELOPMENT OF A LESBIAN-FEMINIST MORALITY

The development of a lesbian community emerged in response to isolation, stigmatization, and oppression stemming from cultural homophobia. For lesbians who had been ostracized from their families of origin, who felt like outsiders within dominant heterosexual culture, and who felt like they were living on the margins of society, the lesbian community created a haven of validation, acceptance and belonging, a "safety zone" which provided a buffer against cultural homophobia and which allowed lesbians to differentiate the allies from the oppressor (M. Hill, personal communication, August 26, 1998). Moreover, lesbian culture offered friendship networks, alternative families, social and political opportunities, and possibilities for intimate and sexual relationships. From the development of lesbian-feminism, a new value system based on the resistance of patriarchy and the empowerment of women and other oppressed groups was established. Had the phenomena of sexism and cultural homophobia gone unnamed and unacknowledged, and had lesbians failed to join together in a collective effort to fight against these injustices, the lesbian community as it exists today would never have come into being. Instead, by naming the oppression that lesbians were experiencing, lesbians were successful in creating a woman-centered community of pride and solidarity.

Yet once the lesbian-feminist community was established, it began to take on a life of its own. Following the traditional paradigm of naming and norming, the act of naming sexism and homophobia led to the formation of a community, the development of group norms, and the establishment of rules. Widespread use of the slogans "the personal is political" and "feminism is the theory, lesbianism is the practice" marked the creation of a lesbian-feminist morality which dictated how lesbians should live their lives. While establishing a lesbian-feminist morality was intended to provide a means of challenging and resisting patriarchal oppression (and to some extent succeeded), this new set of rules ultimately became a list of "shoulds" and "should nots," not unlike the "shoulds" and "should nots" of dominant heterosexual culture. Whereas lesbians had once been excluded from the dominant culture, women who did not live up to lesbian-feminist standards were now denigrated and excluded from the lesbian-feminist community, and their actions were judged to be immoral and unethical (Hoagland, 1988). Thus, what began as empowerment eventually evolved into oppression, much like that of dominant heterosexual culture: "It is apparent from the rigorous specifications a woman must meet before she dare call herself a lesbian that the freedoms proclaimed in the early days of women's liberation have now become tyrannies of their own" (Elliot, 1991, p. 325).

CASUALTIES OF THE LESBIAN-FEMINIST MORALITY: TWO EXAMPLES

While the evolution of a lesbian-feminist moral framework had been in the service of promoting solidarity and combating the effects of patriarchal oppression, it resulted in the construction of a politically correct lesbian identity, suppressing diversity and difference within the lesbian community. Every choice a lesbian made was now a matter of morality, which led to the silencing and ostracism of women who did not fit the politically correct paradigm. Intended to free women from the constraints of dominant heterosexual culture, the "rules" established by the lesbian community, particularly around sexual desire and behavior and physical appearance, created yet another site of oppression for lesbians.

Sexual desire/behavior. One result of naming and acknowledging heteropatriarchal oppression was the formation of a lesbian-separatist community. Because radical lesbian-feminists considered heterosexual relationships to be "the key mechanism of the global phenomenon of male domination, oppression and exploitation of females" (Frye, 1990, cited in Golden, 1994, p. 67), women who identified as feminists were strongly encouraged to relate only to women and to withdraw from their relationships with men as well as from women who continued to relate to men sexually. While this idea was first articulated in the 1970s, this belief is still widespread; as recently as 1990, Marilyn Frye wrote:

> If the institution of female heterosexuality is . . . central to the continuous replication of patriarchy, then women's abandonment

of that institution recommends itself as one strategy (perhaps among others) in the project of dismantling patriarchal structures. (Frye, 1990, cited in Golden, 1994, p. 67)

In addition to relating only to women, lesbians were discouraged from engaging in sexual practices that seemingly replicated the power dynamics of heterosexual relationships, including S/M, butch/femme relationships, and male/female sex.

Lesbian-separatism was undoubtedly an attempt to empower women who violated the rules of compulsory heterosexuality, as well as to encourage social and political solidarity among women. Yet it ultimately resulted in the exclusion, denigration, and pathologizing of women who did not live up to these lesbian-feminist moral standards. Women who identified as feminists and who chose to be involved sexually with men were accused of "sleeping with the enemy" and of betraying the feminist cause. Women who identified as lesbians (not as bisexual) and who continued to have sex with men were seen as thumbing their noses at lesbian-feminists. And women who engaged in S/M were accused of perpetuating female sexual slavery by engaging in abusive and exploitive acts.

While the sexual norms of lesbian-separatists initially created a sense of liberation as well as social and political solidarity among women, eventually it splintered the community by replicating the abuses of power that feminists were originally fighting against. Just as dominant culture had labeled lesbian desire as "wrong" and "immoral," the lesbian-feminist community, by dictating how women should behave sexually, branded bisexuality and alternative sexual practices as "anti-feminist." And just as compulsory heterosexuality within dominant culture rendered lesbianism invisible, the lesbian-feminist definition of sexuality as a strict dichotomy resulted in the invisibility of women who did not fall cleanly into either category. In essence, the creation of moral codes within the lesbian-feminist community, instead of promoting empowerment through political solidarity, ultimately prevented feminists from fully understanding female sexuality, from engaging in a continuous dialogue on power in sexual relationships, and from achieving true sexual liberation.

Physical appearance. In recent years, feminists have made significant strides in politicizing women's dissatisfaction with their bodies and obsession with their weight. Whereas previously eating disorders were viewed as individual pathology, feminists offered an alternative, political conceptualization of eating disorders and body dissatisfaction as epitomizing and reinforcing powerlessness and dependency in women (e.g., Brown, 1985). At the same time, feminists noted that women's energies towards combating oppression were greatly diminished because of this pervasive obsession with achieving the feminine beauty ideal (Wolf, 1991). While feminists, particularly heterosexual feminists, were taking an interest in the politics of thinness and eating disorders, lesbian-feminists approached the issue of body image from a different angle and became much more involved in fat politics. By viewing lesbianism and self-nourishment as equally revolutionary feminist actions, lesbian-feminists called for a reclaiming of both physical and sexual space as a means of subverting the patriarchy (Brown, 1987; Dworkin, 1989).

While naming the political nature of thinness by heterosexual feminists and naming the existence of fat oppression by lesbian feminists were two separate strands in the body image discourse, these two strands intersected in the establishment of appearance norms for lesbians. According to Esther Rothblum (1994), these appearance norms served two functions: to provide a means for lesbians, an often invisible and oppressed group, to identify one another without being identifiable to the dominant culture; and to provide a group identity with separate norms from the dominant culture. With the advent of feminism, lesbian appearance norms evolved as a means of challenging heterosexual standards of beauty and offering an alternative set of standards, freeing women from the constraints of mainstream ideals of beauty.

While these appearance norms were originally aimed at challenging patriarchy and promoting lesbian visibility, they quickly evolved into standards of political correctness that were heavily policed. Lesbians who were more feminine, for example, were viewed as identifying with heterosexual culture and betraying the lesbian-feminist moral framework. These expectations, instead of freeing lesbians from the constraints of female beauty, placed new limitations on how lesbians should appear and thus restricted lesbians' freedom to choose how to appear. Additionally, these standards of appearance placed lesbians in a no-win situation; essentially, lesbians were asked to "rise above" their culture and automatically erase the effects that years of growing up as women in our body-image-obsessed culture had on them, and then lesbians were expected to subscribe to an equally constraining standard of appearance. Hence, lesbian-feminists were saying, "You can choose how you want to look, but you must look like us."

The lesbian-feminist morality on physical appearance also had serious implications with respect to eating disorders among lesbians. Because the discourse on eating disorders and weight preoccupation was focused primarily on heterosexual women and was thus construed as a "straight woman's" problem, lesbian-feminist moral standards led to the silencing of eating disorders and body dissatisfaction within the lesbian community:

> The notion that eating problems are limited to heterosexual women has also contributed to some lesbians' secrecy.... This ... secrecy among lesbians [is] based on the fear of being misunderstood or rejected by other lesbians. The connotation of anorexia and bulimia as problems developed by those who accept male models of beauty means that a lesbian with an eating problem is admitting to being male-centered and therefore not appropriately lesbian. (Thompson, 1994, p. 15)

This silencing of eating disorders, while preserving the stereotype that lesbians are free from the vise-like grip of eating disturbances among women, has serious psychological and political implications for lesbians. Psychologically, in addition to struggling with an eating disorder, lesbians may feel alienated, ashamed, and inadequate as lesbians. Politically, maintaining the silence perpetuates the notion that only heterosexual women have eating disorders and that heterosexual culture is the only culprit, when in actuality the heavy policing of lesbian standards of appearance may also play a role.

Summary. The construction of a lesbian-feminist morality, while initially intended to create solidarity and resistance against patriarchy and compulsory heterosexuality, resulted in the splintering of a community and the undermining of feminist principles. What began as a collective effort to empower women resulted in the creation of a highly policed community, where breaking the rules often resulted in alienation and isolation from the lesbian-feminist community. This alienation had serious implications for women who did not fit the norm in the lesbian-feminist community or within dominant culture, particularly women of color, poor and working class women, multicultural women, and bisexual women. Interestingly, this is very much like the strict policing of compulsory heterosexuality within dominant culture.

Thus, the creation of a lesbian-feminist voice, while making great strides against patriarchy, also created a set of "guilt politics" (Schneider, 1991) which led to the silencing of other voices which could potentially enrich and deepen our feminist consciousness; it has divided women who were initially working towards the same feminist goal; it has undermined the power of personal choice by placing restrictions on individual behaviors; and it has led to burnout and caused activists to drop the feminist cause (Schneider, 1991). What began as an attempt to resist oppression has resulted, in part, in an undermining of the feminist goals that we initially set out to achieve.

NAMING, FEMINISM, AND ETHICAL PRACTICE IN PSYCHOLOGY: SHALL THE TWAIN EVER MEET?

The development of a lesbian-feminist morality, stemming from naming the injustices of sexism and homophobia, is highly relevant for the feminist therapist, for it illustrates how, through the use and misuse of power, feminist naming and morality can evolve into a dialectic between empowerment and subjugation. The power of the therapist lies in her expertise and authority–the expertise to name, label, and categorize the thoughts, feelings, and experiences of the client, and the authority to dictate how they should be handled. However, within mainstream psychology, this power is often used (and abused) to maintain and strengthen power imbalances between clients and therapists; to reinforce the normative standards of dominant culture with regard to normalcy and pathology; and to isolate the individual from his or her multifaceted experience. Psychodiagnosis, "the power to call behavior pathological as opposed to normative" (Brown, 1994, p. 126), is the most common site of this type of abuse of power.

Clearly, the very act of naming poses a number of ethical dilemmas for feminist therapists. Naming is undeniably a politically powerful act, for it is the crucial first step in challenging existing norms, establishing new normative standards, and instilling a new set of moral principles. Yet paradoxically, while naming that which has been obscured and denied is a crucial first step in reclaiming power and effecting political change, naming has the potential to evolve into dogmatism and rhetoric, creating yet another means of social and political control structured on the template of patriarchy. As therapists, naming, labeling, reframing, categorizing, and validating are part of our everyday work. Yet as feminists, we are continually wary of the use of naming, given how it has been used to label and pigeonhole the oppressed. Thus, as feminist therapists, we are constantly engaged in the process of naming while simultaneously challenging this process. Given the clear contradiction between the two, we are caught in a web of deciding how (and whether) we as feminists can use naming as a tool of empowerment rather than a tool of oppression, and, when norms and moral standards arise from naming, whether we as feminist therapists should dictate and enforce feminist morality.

Validating women's diverse experiences and challenging cultural institutions which dominate and control members of oppressed groups are two major goals of feminist therapy and politics. While naming has the potential to contribute to each of these goals, it can also easily contradict and undermine them, for, as seen from the above examples, naming can also evolve into the invalidation of one's identity and experience and the perpetuation of domination and control. Yet ceasing to continue naming injustices for fear of creating oppressive norms and standards of correctness is taking a backward step. Naming is an important tool for feminists; it attributes meaning, legitimacy, and validation to experiences that were previously unacknowledged by dominant culture, and it acts as a starting point for political and social change.

Thus, the question is not *whether* feminist naming can exist, given feminist criticism of traditional uses of naming, but *how* feminists can use naming as a tool for empowering their clients and working towards social change. Mary Ballou (1995) suggests that, through the application of a different world view, a feminist value system, and a clear understanding of the dynamics of power, naming can be a powerful tool used to validate women's experience, acknowledge the impact of the cultural environment, and challenge the tenets of dominant culture. In doing so, feminist therapists must have a thorough awareness and understanding of the power and authority they hold. Clients tend to experience therapists as extremely powerful; they view their therapists as having authority and expertise, and they tend to place value on the expertise of the therapist. As feminist therapists, when we can acknowledge our power and develop an understanding of its therapeutic as well as its exploitive potential, we will be more able to use the power of naming to achieve feminist goals. Without an awareness of the depth and scope of our power, naming is far more likely to evolve into dogmatism used to enforce moral and normative standards, thus encouraging further oppression and subverting feminist challenges to the imbalances of power in dominant culture.

TOWARDS A NEW FEMINIST MORALITY

Despite the tremendous potential for abuses of power, many feminists nevertheless believe that the enforcement of a feminist morality is vital in order to effectively combat oppression. In her reflections on lesbian morality, Nancy Berson (1984), for example, argues that "as Lesbians we must be more morally upright, more honest, more aboveboard in our dealings with each other than our oppressors have been with us" (p. 49). In a similar vein, Celia Kitzinger and Rachel Perkins (1993) argue that "shoulds" and notions of "right" and "wrong" are necessary components of lesbian-feminist morality, and they criticize feminist psychologists for refusing to take an explicit moral stand:

> Nonjudgmentalism, uncritical acceptance of everyone's 'right to her own opinion,' and the bland 'validation' of everyone's disparate experience, does not seem either possible or desirable from a feminist perspective. Feminism is, after all, about choosing to prioritize certain values in our lives and trying to live according to those. Feminism is a *moral* framework; it involves making judgments about right or wrong, good and bad. (Kitzinger and Perkins, 1993, p. 16)

Yet using political correctness as a guiding principle for feminist ethical decision-making results in moral absolutes that mimic the authoritarianism of dominant culture. Moreover, morality based on absolutes excludes and penalizes women who do not fit the normative standards governed by the moral rules. Thus, making judgments based on a set of "rights" and "wrongs," without considering the reasons behind the rules, constrains our thinking by leaving little room for the incorporation of alternative viewpoints, experiences, and perspectives, resulting in exclusion based on privilege, the perpetuation of the moral paradigm of dominant culture, and the undermining of feminist goals.

Given the predilection for feminist morals and ethics to mimic the dynamics of patriarchy, it is vital for feminists to reconceptualize the framework of our morality. Instead of relying on rules and regulations to govern our actions, Sara Lucia Hoagland (1988) and Sue Cartledge (1983) each call for a new feminist morality based on self in relation to the community, weaving together the power of personal choice and creativity with an understanding of how personal choices affect the greater community. This new feminist morality addresses the empowerment that comes through utilizing the full range of choices that we have in our lives, the fact that a restricted range of choices exists for many women, *and* the fact that all of our choices have social and political implications. Additionally, in contrast to the rigidity, inflexibility, and dogmatism of traditional ethics, a morality based on feminist principles must be a constantly developing morality, a work-in-progress.

For example, with respect to feminist therapy, Mary Ballou (1995) suggests that when a behavior does not match a norm, rather than engaging in the rhetoric of "thou shalt and thou shalt not" and attributing deviance to the individual, feminist therapists should instead begin to raise questions about the hidden assumptions and views within the norm itself. Using Ballou's alternative paradigm, instead of blaming and chastizing lesbians who choose to relate to men (both sexually and non-sexually), we can begin to question the rules which govern sexual behavior and examine the assumptions behind these rules, such as the belief that sexual desire fits neatly into a dichotomous paradigm, as well as the notion that lesbian separatism is the only "correct" feminism. And instead of alienating lesbians who defy the appearance norms of the lesbian community, we can begin to challenge the notion that body dissatisfaction is a problem only among heterosexual women, as well as the assumption that a "correct" appearance standard for lesbians is a feminist one. Adopting a questioning stance rather than a castigating one allows for the ongoing development of a complex feminist morality based on diverse personal experience rather than a set of unyielding and potentially oppressive rules. Thus, the focus is shifted from rules to underlying principles, from dogmatism to pluralism, from stagnancy to constant evolution and change, and from conformity and coercion to individual empowerment within the community.

In exploring the possibilities within a new feminist morality, consider the following comments made by Susan Bordo (1993):

> In my view, [feminism] is not a blueprint for the conduct of personal life (or political action, for that matter) and does not empower (or require) individuals to "rise above" their culture or to become martyrs to feminist ideals. It does not tell us what to *do* . . . whether to lose weight or not, wear makeup or not, lift weights or not . . . It is up to the [individual] to decide how, when, and where (or whether) to put that understanding to further use, in the particular, complicated, and ever-changing context that is his or her life and no one else's. (p. 30)

While Bordo was not referring specifically to feminist therapy, her comments are particularly relevant. As therapists, we can use our power and expertise to apply a feminist perspective to each client's experience, and we have the power to help the client identify what the range of choices are. As therapists, we also have the power to influence decision-making through the dictation of a feminist ideology. In adhering to a feminist morality based on ending oppression, as therapists we must critique whether we are using our influence in the service of eliminating oppression or reinforcing dogmatism.

CONCLUSION

The Preamble to the Feminist Therapy Code of Ethics (Feminist Therapy Institute, 1987) states that the code is "a living document and thus is continually in the process of change" (Feminist Therapy Institute, 1987, cited in Rave and Larsen, 1995, p. 39). Likewise, the processes of naming and of practicing within a feminist moral framework can be useful tools in achieving feminist goals only through continuous dialogue, critique, and evaluation of our use of these tools. Through engagement in an ongoing process of challenging and redefining the "rules" of feminism, through the acknowledgement of the tremendous power we have as therapists, and through the use of this power in a positive rather than in an exploitive manner, feminist naming, done within an ever-evolving feminist moral framework, can be exceptionally powerful in challenging and combating institutionalized oppression.

REFERENCES

American Psychiatric Association. (1973). *Diagnostic and Statistical Manual of Mental Disorders, Second Edition (DSM-II)*. Washington, D.C.: American Psychiatric Association.

American Psychiatric Association. (1994). *Diagnostic and Statistical Manual of Mental Disorders, Fourth Edition (DSM-IV)*. Washington, D.C.: American Psychiatric Association.

Ballou, M. (1995). Naming the issue. In E.J. Rave and C.C. Larsen (Eds.), *Ethical Decision Making in Therapy* (pp. 42-56). New York: The Guilford Press.

Berson, N. (1984). On lesbian morality. *Common Lives/Lesbian Lives, 13*, 47-49.

Bordo, S. (1993). *Unbearable Weight: Feminism, Western Culture, and the Body*. Berkeley: University of California Press.

Brown, L.S. (1985). Women, weight, and power: Feminist theoretical and therapeutic issues. *Women & Therapy, 4*(1), 61-71.

Brown, L.S. (1987). Lesbians, weight, and eating: New analyses and perspectives. In Boston Lesbian Psychologies Collective (Eds.), *Lesbian Psychologies* (pp. 294-309). Urbana: University of Illinois Press.

Brown, L.S. (1989). Beyond thou shalt not: Thinking about ethics in the lesbian therapy community. *Women & Therapy, 8*(1-2), 13-26.

Brown, L.S. (1994). *Subversive Dialogues: Theory in Feminist Therapy*. New York: Basic Books.

Cartledge, S. (1983). Duty and desire: Creating a feminist morality. In S. Cartledge and J. Ryan (Eds.), *Sex and Love: New Thoughts on Old Contradictions* (pp. 167-179). London: The Women's Press.

Dworkin, S.H. (1989). Not in man's image: Lesbians and the cultural oppression of body image. *Women & Therapy, 8*(1-2), 27-39.

Elliot, B. (1991). Bisexuality: The best thing that ever happened to lesbian-feminism? In L. Hutchins and L. Kaahumanu (Eds.), *Bi Any Other Name: Bisexual People Speak Out* (pp. 324-328). Los Angeles: Alyson Books.

Feminist Therapy Institute (1987). *Feminist Therapy Code of Ethics*. Denver: Author.

Friedan, B. (1963). *The Feminine Mystique*. New York: Dell Publishing.

Frye, M. (1990). Do you have to be a lesbian to be a feminist? *Off Our Backs*, 21-23.

Golden, C. (1994). Our politics and choices: The feminist movement and sexual orientation. In B. Greene and G.M. Herek (Eds.), *Lesbian and Gay Psychology* (pp. 54-70). Thousand Oaks: Sage Publications.

Herman, J.L. (1992). Complex PTSD: A syndrome in survivors of prolonged and repeated trauma. *Journal of Traumatic Stress, 5*(3), 377-391.

Hoagland, S.L. (1988). *Lesbian Ethics*. Palo Alto: Institute of Lesbian Studies.

Kitzinger, C. and Perkins, R. (1993). *Changing Our Minds: Lesbian Feminism and Psychology*. New York: New York University Press.

Laporte, L. and Guttman, H. (1996). Traumatic childhood experiences as risk factors for borderline and other personality disorders. *Journal of Personality Disorders, 10*(3), 247-259.

Porter, N. (n.d.). Victim blaming through diagnoses. Unpublished manuscript.

Rave, E.J. and Larsen, C. C. (1995). *Ethical Decision Making in Therapy*. New York: The Guilford Press.

Rich, A. (1980). Compulsory heterosexuality and lesbian existence. *Signs, 5*(4), 631-660.

Rothblum, E.D. (1994). Lesbians and physical appearance: Which model applies? In B. Greene and G.M. Herek (Eds.), *Lesbian and Gay Psychology* (pp. 84-97). Thousand Oaks: Sage Publications.

Schneider, A. (1991). Guilt politics. In L. Hutchins and L. Kaahumanu (Eds.), *Bi Any Other Name: Bisexual People Speak Out* (pp. 275-278). Los Angeles: Alyson Books.

Thompson, B.W. (1994). *A Hunger So Wide and So Deep*. Minneapolis: University of Minnesota Press.

Tiefer, L. (1988). A feminist critique of the sexual dysfunction nomenclature. *Women & Therapy, 7*(2/3), 5-22.

Weaver, T.L. and Clum, G.A. (1993). Early family environments and traumatic experiences associated with borderline personality disorder. *Journal of Consulting and Clinical Psychology, 61*(6), 1068-1075.

Wolf, N. (1991). *The Beauty Myth*. New York: Doubleday.

Zetlin, P. (1989). A proposal for a new diagnostic category: Abuse disorder. *Journal of Feminist Family Therapy, 1*(4), 67-83.

What Is Necessary, and What Is Right? Feminist Dilemmas in Community Mental Health

Lynda L. Warwick

SUMMARY. Feminist therapists value the empowerment of clients and the appropriate sharing of the therapist's institutionalized power. As therapists who are also "mandated reporters," we are obligated under certain circumstances to use our power to warn potential victims of harm, to prevent clients from harm to self or others, or make reports to institutions which have a great impact on clients' lives. Using four case examples, this paper will present clinical situations where the use of the therapist's power interfaces with homophobia, racism, and paternalism in the lives of low-income clients. *[Article copies available for a fee from The Haworth Document Delivery Service: 1-800-342-9678. E-mail address: getinfo@haworthpressinc.com]*

KEYWORDS. Feminist, ethical, moral, clinical, therapy

As feminist therapists, we come to our work with varying systems of belief which provide personal and professional moral guidance.

Lynda L. Warwick, PhD, is Director of Outpatient Therapy at the Greater Lawrence Mental Health Center.

Address correspondence to: Lynda L. Warwick, Greater Lawrence Mental Health Center, 30 General Street, Lawrence, MA 01841-2961 (E-mail: lwarwick@juno.com).

[Haworth co-indexing entry note]: "What Is Necessary, and What Is Right? Feminist Dilemmas in Community Mental Health." Warwick, Lynda L. Co-published simultaneously in *Women & Therapy* (The Haworth Press, Inc.) Vol. 22, No. 2, 1999, pp. 39-51; and: *Beyond the Rule Book: Moral Issues and Dilemmas in the Practice of Psychotherapy* (eds: Ellyn Kaschak, and Marcia Hill) The Haworth Press, Inc., 1999, pp. 39-51. Single or multiple copies of this article are available for a fee from The Haworth Document Delivery Service [1-800-342-9678, 9:00 a.m. - 5:00 p.m. (EST). E-mail address: getinfo@haworthpressinc.com].

Some of us are guided by religious backgrounds, others from humanistic, political, or other philosophical perspectives. We have our own ideas about what is "right," what is "just," and how we should act in situations where our values are challenged. This is particularly important because, as therapists, our actions, interventions and decisions often have a concrete impact on clients' lives. Because we are granted institutionalized power in order to safeguard the welfare of our clients, our professions provide us with ethical systems which are designed to help us make decisions about the most appropriate use of our conferred power. We also share, as feminists, a commitment to the empowerment of our clients. We are committed to the use of our institutionalized power in a way which increases the options for clients to make choices about their own lives, and which decreases the impact of large systems which may not have the best interest of our clients at heart. Ideally these interlocking systems of morals and ethics work together smoothly. We can use our conferred power to advocate for a client, to teach a client to advocate for herself and her family, and there is no conflict between our personal beliefs about what is right, our professional standards as embodied in the ethical principles, and our commitment as feminists to the empowerment of clients. Sometimes, however, those systems may be in conflict. Particularly in situations where we are required as "mandated reporters" to make choices with which we may not be personally comfortable, we may find that what is ethical may not seem to be what is right. In this paper, I will present several examples where the struggle among systems of moral and ethical guidance is significant.

I am a psychologist, an administrator, a white, middle-class lesbian. I work in a mental health center where most clients are poor and the majority are Hispanic. The differential in power between my clients and me is significant. I have enough money, good health care, a quiet, safe living situation, reliable transportation, and educational credentials which give me the chance to maintain my status. I also have some power to make decisions about policies and procedures which affect the therapists and clients in the agency. When I sit in my office with a client, I am often facing someone who has none of these advantages. Clients have to face problems related to poverty, racism, domestic violence, unsafe housing, poor health, language and immigration barriers, and lack of education as well as whatever issues have brought them to therapy. Psychosis, a history of severe trauma, disabling depression or anxiety and substance abuse mean that clients must face serious environmental and social problems with additional personal stresses and without the institutionalized power that I have. In addition, most of my clients are negotiating their way through a network of social service agencies which are designed to meet their needs but which are often clogged with bureaucracy.

My moral foundation comes from my religious beliefs, which are based in feminist earth-based spirituality. This religious framework informs me that my work must not harm others, that I should not use my power in a manipulative way, and that I should support self-determination. This religious perspective places significant emphasis on the role of personal responsibility in making decisions about how to use power in relation to other people. I believe that while good clinical work may sometimes hurt, it should not harm; it should not cause more problems or damage for the client than it solves. I believe in clients' right to self-determination, even as I am aware that those rights are sometimes severely impinged upon by the larger social systems in which they live, such as families, social service systems, work environments, and the political environment which may control many of their choices. I also believe that, in general, it is best to comply with professional codes of ethics (APA, 1990) and to seek ways to comply which do not harm the best interests of clients.

The decision to act in compliance with professional codes of ethics is an individual one. I choose to follow the codes in order to protect myself and my clients, which I believe is one way of minimizing the potential harm that my work could otherwise cause. The guidelines, while not perfect, are designed to help therapists make decisions in the best interests of clients. Therapists have sometimes argued that there are "good clinical reasons" for rejecting the ethical code's restrictions, particularly in regard to sexual contact with current or past clients, but in many cases the "good clinical reasons" turn out to be what the therapist wants to do to meet his or her own needs at the expense of clients. Other cases are less clear-cut; the ethical code requirements may seem to be in conflict with the best interests of the client. As I will show, in general when I have run into such situations I do my best to find a way to follow the ethical code which makes sense clinically and which is acceptable in terms of what I believe is morally right.

As a feminist therapist, I have a moral imperative to engage with my clients in ways which increase their ability to get and use power for their own benefit and for the benefit of those in their social environment, such as partners, family members, or the social group with which they identify. I may do this through various modalities of therapy, through teaching self-advocacy, through education about racism, classism, and sexism as it applies to particular clients, and through a careful monitoring of my work to make certain that I use my influence and advocacy only when clients cannot effectively advocate for themselves. I use my power as a therapist to advocate for clients with their insurance companies, the courts or social service agencies, always being clear with clients what I am doing and how and why.

Most of the time, the moral imperative to use institutionally granted power for the empowerment of clients is in alignment with professional codes of ethics. Talking with a suicidal client about a voluntary hospital stay allows the locus of control to remain with the client, as much as possible. Making a necessary care and protection report in the presence of an overwhelmed parent who realizes the need for help allows the client at least to know fully what is happening and why. Informing a violent client of my duty to warn a potential victim under certain circumstances or reviewing limits of confidentiality empowers a client because I am clear about what my limits are; the client can then make decisions about how to behave and what to disclose to me. If the client knows under what circumstances I will have to use my power in ways they would not prefer, the choice becomes theirs about whether to put the two of us in that position.

However, there are circumstances where what is right seems to be in partial conflict with what is necessary. There are situations in which the moral imperative to use power for the empowerment of clients makes it difficult to act in ways which are ethical and/or mandated by law (General Law of Massachusetts, 1991). Perhaps there are ways in which we can minimize the use of institutionalized power against the will of clients, and methods for working through the situations where we must do what is necessary even though it may not seem morally right. To do this, I will use case examples which are composites of clients I have worked with. Identifying information has been changed, and some situations may combine the experiences of several clients in order to make the moral dilemma clear.

Maria is a divorced heterosexual Hispanic woman in her 50s, with four grown children and severe, chronic depression. Fifteen years of therapy and psychopharmacological interventions have not significantly relieved the pain of her depression, which is complicated by poor health, low income, and a history of severe trauma which produces intrusive symptoms. Although Maria and I have a strong therapeutic alliance, she is frequently on the edge of suicide. Under no circumstances will Maria consider psychiatric hospitalization, after a previous experience demonstrated to her that hospitalization increased her feelings of powerlessness and alienation. Maria has a multitude of suicide plans, refuses to remove the means to carry out these plans from her home, and knows that as long as she denies intent to act on her suicidal ideation, it would be difficult to commit her under involuntary commitment statutes. Maria expresses a heartfelt wish to die, but reports that she does not wish to burden her adult children with the stigma of having their mother commit suicide. However, most times she is at moderate to high risk of acting on her suicidal ideation. Maria sometimes says that she relies on my sense of hope that her life can improve, but more often she tells me that what she wants is for me to help her plan for a dignified death, with a minimal impact on her family. She wishes I could help her explain her decision to die to her family, to help her access medications which will assure a painless death, and to support her as she lets go of life in preparation for suicide.

I believe that Maria has the right to self-determination, and I can understand what she wants me to help her do and why. However, there are complicated moral and ethical reasons why I cannot do what she wants me to do. First of all, I am morally committed to see that my work does not cause harm. I believe that Maria wants relief from her pain and a better quality of life; she sees suicide as the best way to relieve her pain, but my job is to help her identify other ways of reducing her pain and improving her life. I have to accept the responsibility for believing that what Maria says she wants is not what she truly wants, or at least not what is in her best interest. Perhaps this is patronizing, but there is some evidence for this belief in that Maria faithfully attends sessions and does sometimes say she relies on my sense of hope for her. In minimizing the harm that my work with Maria does, I have to come to some resolution about what that means for my belief in her right to self-determination.

According to the ethical code of my profession, as well as the laws of my state, if I have reason to believe that in any given instance Maria is likely to act on her plans, I must initiate involuntary commitment proceedings, regardless of how I feel about the usefulness of hospitalization for her. We discuss this necessity frequently and explicitly, and I have acted on it in the past, with consequences for our relationship and to Maria's sense of trust, safety and control. My moral imperative is to use my power as a licensed psychologist to increase Maria's self-efficacy and empowerment. Maria's morality places significant importance on the feelings of her children, and she wishes that I could help her work with them to accept her commitment to suicide. My inability and unwillingness to do that causes her pain and frustration, and leads to her feeling helpless and controlled by the institutionalized system of ethics to which I subscribe.

What is necessary in this clinical situation, and what is right? Clearly, I must use all means necessary to find ways to relieve Maria's pain so that she will have less of a drive to end her suffering. We have used peer and expert consultation, psychiatric consultation, referrals to support groups, bibliotherapy, and techniques of contemporary trauma therapy. If these fail, and if Maria communicates to me a clear intent to act on her suicidal impulses, it will be ethically necessary for me to send the police and/or an ambulance to her home or place of work or to require her to be evaluated by our emergency team. Hospitalization may preserve Maria's life in a crisis long enough for us to continue to try to find a way to mediate her pain, but it is not what she wants. Is there a way in which such measures can be right? If I believe Maria has the right to end her life, how can I conduct my work in such a way that it becomes very difficult for her to explore her feelings about doing so?

In order to keep the locus of power and control in Maria's hands as much as the ethical code will permit, we rely on careful, clear, frequent communication and on prevention of the states of vulnerability which bring Maria closest to the edge of acting on her impulses, and thus the risk of committal. I encourage Maria to learn as much as she can about her illness, about the range of options for her care, and coach her in advocating for herself with her psychiatrist and with me. I agree to accept her verbal commitment to remain safe, let her know when I am not feeling secure with her ability to maintain a verbal contract, and together we work toward reducing her pain, supporting her endurance, and reducing her vulnerability to impulsive action. I accept Maria's wish to die and acknowledge that I am choosing to act in compliance with the ethical code and that therefore I am not free to support her in that wish, regardless of my empathy for her suffering. I continue to provide hope, offer alternatives, and strengthen her endurance. I meet with her children at her request, to help them understand the depth of her pain and the nature of her struggle. I communicate my perception of her strengths and reasons for her to continue the struggle. And at least once a month, we discuss the fact that while the final decision is hers, if she says or does particular things, I remain committed to acting on the ethical imperative to hospitalize her involuntarily. Neither of us is happy with this reality, but it is one that is inextricably woven into this complex therapy relationship. I am acting in an ethically appropriate fashion, but in doing so I am interfering with Maria's right to decide what she would like my expert help with. I will help her learn to access her power, but not to do what she wants to do. I will do what I can to prevent the harm of suicide, but in doing so I may be harming Maria's sense of efficacy and power, when she already feels powerless. I can frame what I do in terms of providing a safe holding environment, acting as an ethical, responsible professional, or acting from a moral perspective which rejects suicide, but the complexities remain. In affirming my commitment to recovery and life, I am acting in a way which is ethically appropriate and which feels in some ways morally right, but I am aware that the conflict remains.

Jesse is an Anglo mother of four young children, who is newly exploring her lesbian identity in the context of a chaotic, tumultuous relationship. Her three oldest children are in foster care, due to Jesse's physical abuse of them at times in her life when she felt overwhelmed. Slowly she has worked to treat her depression and trauma, to hold a job, and to reduce the intensity of her relationships with her lover and with her children's fathers. We work on what being lesbian means for her, and I encourage her to learn through reading and through meeting other women what life as a lesbian might hold for her. Much of our work involves exploring how she can stabilize her life and relationship while continuing the process of identifying as lesbian. One day, she mentions that her Protective Services worker might call me to ask how her therapy is going. "Don't tell her I'm a lesbian, okay? I'm afraid I won't get my kids back." Jesse knows that she is not ready to have her kids back with her, but does not want to risk closing the door permanently if her worker acts on homophobic perceptions of her fitness to parent.

What is necessary? According to ethical and legal standards, my duty to protect Jesse's confidentiality means that I may release only what she gives me permission to release. Morally, I am committed to using my power to help Jesse use her own, to support her self-determination, and to cause no harm in the course of our work. I have a responsibility to advocate in her best interest, and also to use my power as evaluator in the interest of those she loves, her children and her lover. I have a responsibility to maintain honesty and integrity in my professional communications with her other providers, because morally I believe that dishonesty is generally harmful to me, to other providers and to my client even if it might be convenient. I know that homophobia is certainly present within social service agencies, and I do not believe that her sexuality detracts from her ability to parent. How can I communicate clearly and honestly with the Protective Services worker within the bounds of Jesse's limits, in such a way that her interests are best served? Would it be better if I agreed not to mention her sexuality, to lie if the worker asked directly about her intimate relationships? What is likely to cause the least harm, to be most empowering for Jesse, and to result in the greatest range of choices for her to make?

I meet with Jesse, and tell her my concerns. I tell her that I would like to give her worker an accurate picture of the work she has done to reduce the chaos in her life, so that the worker will be able to make an informed decision about when and how to return her children to her care. I ask Jesse to tell me what she would like her life to look like when it would be time for her children to return. Together we outline a life that includes stable employment, a sense of clarity and comfort with her identity as a lesbian, a consistent and significant improvement in her depression, and a reliable, non-abusive partner. We decide that, because most of these conditions are not yet met, it is not necessary that I discuss her identity development as a lesbian with her worker. I am able to communicate the areas where Jesse sees a need for improvement to the worker and to give a clear picture of her ability to parent on a limited basis, without putting her at risk of institutionalized homophobia. Later, as she becomes more clear about her identity and begins to practice coming out to family and friends, she may be more able to talk with her worker in a way which conveys a sense of pride, health and stability. She may also have access by then to a network of social support which could help her if the institutionalized homophobia within the Department of Social Services causes problems for her and her family. I believe that honesty and self-disclosure under appropriate circumstances are likely to lead to the best outcome for Jesse, because I believe that living honestly within a supportive community is better than living in fear, dishonesty, and isolation. However, we have a moral responsibility to decide what constitutes the most appropriate circumstances for disclosure in order to prevent the harm of premature disclosure.

As the personal is political in the therapy room, so the political becomes personal. In these days of mergers, managed care, and limitations on therapy, developments in the insurance industry or Medicaid legislation can have a direct impact on the way agencies function and the kind of care clients may receive. As agencies struggle to survive, free care money disappears, minimum fees for therapy grow, and every therapy hour must be billable. As feminist therapists, how can we use our power to advocate for clients' access to therapy?

Jeff has been a client of the agency for fifteen years. He has bipolar disorder and PTSD from a childhood and adolescence of violence. He has made three serious suicide attempts and comes to the agency primarily for the medications which stabilize his mood somewhat. On the recommendation of his long-time psychiatrist, Jeff agrees to see an individual therapist. He and I establish a therapeutic relationship and begin to work at stabilizing his moods, improving his relationships, keeping his job, and, as it becomes relevant, we begin to question some of the beliefs his history has left him with. After two years, Jeff changes jobs and begins to work in a setting which is much better for him. His insurance plan changes. I am no longer covered.

Jeff declares that he will not transfer to another therapist and becomes suicidal as his mood drops. Gently, I begin to explore options for transfer with him, offering to talk with therapists who can accept his insurance, hold a joint meeting, write a referral letter outlining the issues he has been working on. Jeff says that he has had other therapists in the past and has not been able to make progress with them. He believes that there is something about me, rather than something different in his condition, which has made it possible for him to begin to make progress in changing his life, and he may be right. He refuses to transfer, and says that he will stay at the agency for his medication management, but will not continue in therapy. His insurance benefits have run out, which means that his medication management may not be covered anymore. Meanwhile, he becomes increasingly depressed and angry.

The agency has a minimum fee of $75/hour, and no provision for free care. Jeff petitions his insurance company for an extension of benefits, with my help, and is turned down on the grounds that, since it has been four years since his last suicide attempt, he is not at sufficient risk to justify continued benefits. He considers changing jobs, but the job he currently has is a step up from previous jobs, and it has many advantages for him. He advocates for himself as much as he can, but he has little education, no access to a word processor or the internet, and has enough to do managing his symptoms.

The agency is in serious financial trouble, and there are those who believe that clients must bear part of the burden of the times. If we refer him to a local agency with a lower minimum fee, we have done our job, and it is up to him to decide whether to continue with therapy or not. However, there are others who believe we have an obligation to long-term clients. What is necessary? What is right?

The chief administrator, the medical director, the billing manager and I meet and I present the case. We discuss Jeff's long history with the clinic and with his psychiatrist, the fact that he has always paid his part of the fee, the fact that he is possibly at risk of suicide given his history and his current depression. We decide to arrange an affordable fee agreement for Jeff, assuming the loss as an agency, until such time as he decides to change jobs, regains the next years' benefits, or changes insurance plans. The medical director and I will continue to advocate for Jeff with his insurance company on grounds of medical necessity. We have enough evidence to support a justification of avoiding abandonment of a client at risk. I am able to advocate for such a step because I believe that it supports Jeff's right to self-determination and that to refuse to advocate for him would cause harm to him. The power of the agency, moderated through my power as a therapist, is made available to the client so that he can make a decision about his care. He may choose not to accept a fee agreement, even if it is one he can afford, and may decide to terminate therapy.

Lourdes is a 53 year old woman who moved to the mainland from Puerto Rico at the age of 14. She married Papi at 17, a man from Puerto Rico who has abused her sexually, physically, emotionally and financially throughout their long marriage. She worked as a hotel manager as long as she could, but eventually succumbed to the long-term stress and was forced to apply for disability benefits. Papi speaks little English and does not read or write. Lately he has begun to use crack and to beat her. Lourdes is raising her ten-year-old granddaughter and is afraid for both their safety. She is unwilling to request a restraining order because she is afraid of the racism she knows is part of the police force and the criminal justice system in the city. She is unwilling to ask him to leave because she knows he cannot support himself with his lack of skills. She is unwilling to leave because it has been her money which bought the apartment in which they live, as well as all the furnishings. She will not go to a shelter because she is uncomfortable with the lack of Spanish-speaking staff and, on the other hand, is afraid that word will get around the close-knit Puerto Rican community of the trouble in her family. Lourdes begins to sleep with a knife beneath her pillow, and is clear that she will use it if Papi attacks her while he is high.

According to the ethical and legal standards in my state, the duty to break confidentiality and to warn is triggered if there is an identifiable victim, an available means of harm, and the immediate intent to harm. Lourdes has an available weapon, an identified victim, and the intent to harm. All that is missing is the immediate threat to Papi. I begin to talk with Lourdes about my duty to warn Papi if I believe he is at risk from her violence. She begs me not to say anything to him, believing he will harm her before she can defend herself. I think she is probably right. My warning to Papi may result in serious harm to Lourdes, and it is against what she wants. If I choose to use my institutionalized power to carry out a duty to warn, it may go against what I believe is morally right. It also seems wrong not to intervene in a situation which is so dangerous for Lourdes, but at what point do I decide when I have to take the choice out of her hands?

Ethically, I must determine the immediacy of risk to Papi's safety and, if I determine that it is high, I must warn him, inform the police of the risk, or both. I determine that she has no intent to harm him unless he attacks her and she believes her life is in danger. However, that could happen at any time even if she contracts with me not to act on her plans or agrees to get rid of the knife. I decide that in the absence of a clear-cut duty, I will go with my moral perspective, which is that Lourdes should retain as much control over her life as she can.

We decide that neither of us wants to be in a position where Papi must be warned, and we start to think of ways in which Lourdes can protect herself without an immediate threat to Papi's safety. We discuss her role as matriarch of her extended family, and as her granddaughter's guardian. Lourdes decides to share with her extended family the threat she feels from Papi when he is high on crack, and with my encouragement the family creates a plan for Lourdes' protection if she should feel at risk. She decides to send her granddaughter to live with an aunt for the time being. With other members of the family present, she confronts Papi and takes away his house key. Lourdes will control her space by deciding whether it is safe to let Papi in, and will call family members if she becomes afraid. She also plans how and where she will escape if his violence reappears. Lourdes wishes that Papi would get treatment for his substance abuse, but she cannot require him to do so. She tells me that in the past his experiences with substance abuse have usually been short episodes and that she chooses to wait him out. She does, however, remove the knife from under her pillow.

I wish that Lourdes would move on to a life without Papi and his abuse and I worry about her safety and the level of risk she continues to live with. I have made the decision that in this situation I must refrain from using institutionalized power if I am to be most effective in empowering Lourdes. She has the right to make her own decisions, to solve her own problems in her own way, and if there is no immediate threat to herself, to Papi or to her granddaughter I will respect those rights. I can research local women's shelters for her, to find out which have Spanish-speaking staff and which will provide transportation or relocation if she decides to choose those options. I can recommend support groups for battered women and find resources in Spanish for her. I can work to increase her self-esteem and to help her identify alternatives to her current life. But the final decisions about Lourdes' life belong to her.

When the ethical and legal requirements in a given clinical situation seem to conflict with what we believe is morally right, there are no simple or painless solutions. If we believe in empowering clients, we must teach them how to access the power to moderate the impact of such forces as racism, classism, homophobia, and paternalism within the mental health system as well as within their wider social context. We must also make certain that our use of power is consistent with the goal of empowerment for clients, especially in situations where the requirements of the ethical codes may seem to suggest actions which may disempower clients. In such situations, disclosing our ethical responsibility to act may be the first step toward helping clients generate their own solutions so that we avoid having to use our power in ways that clients do not want us to. As feminist therapists, we use the existence and nature of power differentials in therapy as teaching tools–we demonstrate in a clear way that there are differentials in power and that clients can sometimes access power of their own to maintain control over their lives.

The challenge of feminist therapy in the context of ethical dilemmas is that we must find ways to satisfy our moral and ethical mandates while using our institutionalized power for the empowerment of our clients. This often requires some ingenuity and flexibility on the part of therapists and sometimes clients as well. What is ethical is not always easy to sort out, although the ethical codes are tools of our professions that we strive to master. What is right is determined by our morals, our own sense of what is right, and the ways in which we choose to use our power as professionals. As individuals we need to be clear with ourselves, our colleagues, and when appropriate our clients, about what we believe to be morally right. This is part of the disclosure of our values which feminist therapists advocate. Through continual communication with clients and clarification of our roles, we can maintain ethical standards. Through being clear about the power we have, our responsibility to use it, and ways in which we can transfer or share some of our power with clients, we can do what is morally right. As feminist therapists, if we are careful, perhaps we can do both most of the time.

REFERENCES

American Psychological Association. (1990). Ethical principles of psychologists (Amended June 2, 1989). *American Psychologist, 45*, 390-395.

Official Edition of the General Laws of Massachusetts (1991). Boston, MA: West Publishing.

Fragmentation and Integrity: The Search for a Moral Compass While Working as a Therapist Within the Child Welfare System

Sharla Kibel

SUMMARY. Feminist therapy sensitizes our awareness to what is absent and unvoiced. Youngsters in the Child Welfare system are particularly vulnerable to fragmented and disconnected attempts to conceptualize their difficulties, meet their needs, and make decisions about their future. Unprocessed pain and competing agendas generate moral dilemmas that affect information sharing, placement recommendations or the process of uncovering a more complex truth. Therapists have to select from among the roles of advocate, expert or interpreter. Case examples and creative interpretation of a biblical text are used to delineate a moral stance that counters fragmentation by bringing integrity into awareness and action. *[Article copies available for a fee from The Haworth Document Delivery Service: 1-800-342-9678. E-mail address: getinfo@haworthpress inc.com]*

Sharla Kibel, MS, Licensed Marriage, Family and Child Counselor, is employed by the Mental Health Department in Santa Clara County, California. She is a member of the Association for Women in Psychology and Feminist Therapy Institute. She is the parent of two young daughters and considers herself a post-denominational Jew who freely draws from ancient and modern sources that illuminate spiritual and moral discourse.

The author would like to acknowledge Lin Colavin and Ellyn Kaschak for challenging her to keep reaching for clarity as this paper unfolded.

Address correspondence to: Sharla Kibel, 17759 Navajo Trail, Los Gatos, CA 95033. (E-mail: omskibel@inow.com).

[Haworth co-indexing entry note]: "Fragmentation and Integrity: The Search for a Moral Compass While Working as a Therapist Within the Child Welfare System." Kibel, Sharla. Co-published simultaneously in *Women & Therapy* (The Haworth Press, Inc.) Vol. 22, No. 2, 1999, pp. 53-68; and: *Beyond the Rule Book: Moral Issues and Dilemmas in the Practice of Psychotherapy* (eds: Ellyn Kaschak, and Marcia Hill) The Haworth Press, Inc., 1999, pp. 53-68. Single or multiple copies of this article are available for a fee from The Haworth Document Delivery Service [1-800-342-9678, 9:00 a.m. - 5:00 p.m. (EST). E-mail address: getinfo@haworthpressinc.com].

© 1999 by The Haworth Press, Inc. All rights reserved.

KEYWORDS. Integrity as moral guideline, Child Welfare system, morality, feminist therapy

One's moral responsibility as a therapist is accentuated when dealing with clients lacking power in our society. Thus, working with children and adolescents poses unique challenges. Schuchman (1997) points out problems with applying traditional approaches that emphasize the therapist in the role of expert and diagnostician to adolescents, while neglecting adolescents' fluctuating capacities for competence and strength. This mirrors the vulnerability that women and other minorities experience as a result of having the distress arising from power imbalances given pathological and disempowering labels. When such youngsters have suffered abuse that leads to loss of familial caregivers, their vulnerability is extreme. Clinicians in community mental health agencies are increasingly treating such youngsters whose lives are under the supervision of Child Welfare authorities.

Anderson (1997) refers to the "power holders" who may have well-intentioned agendas toward children and adolescents but are liable to project inappropriate needs into their decisions "about what's best for the child" (p. 2). In the Child Welfare system, the need to be seen as appropriately protecting youngsters, as well as the adversarial legal system that is often mobilized, combine to limit sensitive responsiveness to the larger family, community and cultural context. Acting responsibly toward the larger context becomes more complicated when one experiences only selected members of the family or community to which a youngster belongs. As a therapist serving both the children and the decision-makers in the Child Welfare system, one needs to stay alert to the missing pieces of the puzzles presented for diagnosis and treatment. Hubner and Wolfson (1996) describe eloquently how "the life of a 'systems' child . . . has a 'Rashomon' quality. Isolated by the laws of confidentiality, she can never be fully known" (p. 100). Multiple professionals working independently are assigned to "fix" or oversee different aspects of her life.

The Child Welfare system is an organized, legal response to the ancient realities of pain and abuse in families. However, giving power over vulnerable children to judges, social workers, and foster families only places youngsters in a widening web of imperfect and potentially harmful relationships. In these circumstances, nurturing a youngster's growth and development requires a capacity for sensitive damage control.

ABOUT MY BACKGROUND

I was transferred to the Children's Shelter mental health program on returning from maternity leave with my first child. It is significant to me that I began working primarily with youngsters as I began my life as a parent. As a parent and a therapist I think of stewardship, the process of removing or diminishing obstacles to growth, as a core value. It is extremely painful, as a therapist, to stay connected to all the obstacles and losses embedded in this context while staying focused on supporting young people. Their development and growth are distorted, but not halted, by the dislocations they have suffered. However, even in an environment of deprivation and dislocation, I am moved by witnessing how these children unfold. I'm consistently struck by their resilience and capacity to be agents of their own lives.

As a white, Jewish woman who was raised in apartheid South Africa, I have heightened sensitivity to fragmentation and to being defined as both an insider and an outsider in different contexts. All the clients I describe below are of Mexican-American background. While I have taken intensive Spanish courses and have experienced some of the dislocations and insecurities of the immigration experience, I come from a middle-class background and have neither experienced comparable economic insecurities nor color-based racism. As a Jewish woman, I resonate with a culture that emphasizes intense and often anxious interconnection between family members.

Both my Jewish education and my engagement with feminist psychology have influenced the importance I give to issues of visibility and invisibility. I often struggle to bring the truth of my experience into awareness. The challenge lies in making visible what is not accepted or reflected in the shared narratives of mainstream culture. Thus, in exploring a moral framework for decision making, I was drawn to a biblical text, "Do not put a stumbling block in the path of a blind man . . . ." In a context of fragmentation, this provides a template for noticing contextual gaps that need to be bridged by caregivers in order to do a youngster justice. This injunction also speaks to the importance of making visible underlying agendas that may constitute some danger to the young person.

There is a tradition of talmudic and rabbinical commentary that gives value to an ongoing deepening and expanding of a moral principle by concrete case discussion. This is an interesting intersection of talmudic and feminist tradition to which I hope to contribute in my case explorations below.

A CONTEXT OF LOSS AND DISLOCATION

This paper will examine moral and ethical concerns within a community mental health clinic in Santa Clara County, California, that is intended to serve children in protective custody who are being evaluated or placed by the Child Welfare system. We function on the campus of a Children's Shelter within a web of agencies, including the on-site school, the child care workers, the children's legal representatives, investigating social workers, foster families, medical services, etc.

Resources are limited and a child's stay in the shelter can often evoke or exacerbate difficulties and symptoms. Children and adolescents may experience relief, but also extreme feelings of dislocation. They are removed from situations considered sufficiently neglectful or abusive to warrant further investigation, but they do not necessarily have a sense of hope for improved conditions. As a therapist one sees the effects both of harmful family situations and of the trauma of adjusting to a strange institution. The damage is still running its course and the attempted remedies frequently are experienced as even more disorganizing. (An example: I instituted a group for 11 to 14 year old girls with a history of sexual abuse. I discovered, to my surprise, that frustration at the obstacles to being returned to their families preoccupied them significantly more than the aftermath of abuse they had experienced.)

The overriding quality one experiences is fragmentation. This is apparent in the youngsters' experience of themselves, in their being wrenched away from their families, and in the way different systems try to meet their needs in disconnected ways. Youngsters, in turn, act out their well-founded distrust that their needs will be understood or met. Often one feels like the "client" is the agency that wants a more controllable child.

SYSTEMIC SOURCES OF FRAGMENTATION

Adults with responsibilities for these children and adolescents interact with them in compartmentalized ways. Family members are often supervised on visits and prohibited from discussing "the case." Child care staff, who supervise and co-ordinate daily activities, work in shifts. Caseloads are high and crisis situations, such as violent, suicidal or oppositional behaviors, absorb available resources. Institutional structures make it difficult to accomplish goals of information exchange, continuity and consistency. Investigating social workers are bound by meeting legal justifications for depriving parents of custody. After disposition, a new placement worker has to re-familiarize herself with the case and may need very different information.

Defining roles and boundaries has to be a flexible and thoughtful process. A therapist may be called on to be a troubleshooter for crises, a play therapist, a group facilitator, an advocate, an interpreter, an educator/consultant, a mediator, an expert witness, source of recommendations, etc. It feels dangerously easy to collude with destructive systems that inevitably emerge out of the unprocessed pain permeating what should be a safe and healing environment. An instance of this is the urgency one feels to tackle crises while avoiding considered systemic intervention. The pain of employing one's limited resource in the face of bottomless need can lead one either to over-compartmentalize and miss essential elements of how to intervene usefully or, by contrast, to over-function and deprive youngsters or their caregivers of power they do possess.

The processes of fragmentation in response to pain are further expanded by Kagan and Schlosberg (1989) who delineate how "interactions among children, parents, practitioners, and state authorities become fixed through repetitive crises . . . and efforts to determine a narrow cause of problems or focus of blame" (p. 113). Such fixed roles function so as to avoid painful awareness of how all parties participate in maintaining problems. They suggest the importance of taking actions that lead to "sharing the pain" (p. 170) so that the momentum of potential growth is not overridden by the resignation, blaming or hopelessness of players in the disconnected roles of therapist, social worker, parent, etc.

INTEGRITY AS A MORAL DIMENSION

In a context of loss where different outcomes of one's decisions can be equally painful, the Hippocratic edict, "Do No Harm," becomes particularly poignant. For example, courts and social workers struggling to balance the value of preserving families against the dangers to a child's development from abusive homes regularly ask psychological evaluators to assess minors (and sometimes their caretakers) for a mental disorder and to link this to placement recommendations. No matter how well a client's functioning is understood and described, there is no risk-free position to take with regard to the recommendations flowing from one's analysis. Ideally one would encounter one's client free of external agendas. In reality, there are always competing agendas regarding the well-being of minors, not least of which is the wish of a therapist to reduce a youngster's pain. It then becomes all too easy to succumb to delusions of saviorhood which can lead to a dangerous narrowing of perspective, focus and action.

What moral compass, then, can one draw on to guide one through the quest to minimize harm? Leviticus 19 contains commandments and precepts pertaining to holiness (Kedoshim) or goodness. One of these is the Golden Rule. Leviticus 19:14 contains the injunction, "Do not put a stumbling block in front of a blind man." This is found among other warnings not to take advantage of someone's handicap. Rabbinical commentators have developed this concept with broad interpretations that offer some pertinent moral philosophy. How does one evaluate such a source of moral guidance? Abrams (1995) explains how power and authority derived from the perceived virtue of a sage (p. 86). This is how women who lacked overt authority come to be quoted in the commentaries. Therefore a moral compass deriving from carefully debated case examples and commentators respected for character as well as intellect, has good provenance.

Telushkin (1991) explains that "blind" is taken to refer to "anyone who is blind in the matter at hand," making it "one of the hardest commandments never to violate" (p. 498). Thus anyone in a position to give advice has to ensure that it is to the benefit of the recipient rather than to further an agenda unknown to the recipient. Leibowitz (1986), a recently departed and respected female Torah scholar, explains that the reference to fearing God that follows this injunction is a reminder that one has to look to one's conscience (or one's commitment to good) rather than to a court of law or witnesses when attempting to determine how closely one has followed this precept. Legal and ethical guidelines are often inadequate alone, especially in an arena where conflicting approaches can all be given ethical justifications. When one applies such guidelines thoughtfully, rather than reflexively, one is grappling to hold a totality of ramifications and of people deserving consideration in one's awareness. Thus, a moral approach to supporting a youngster and her family would integrate awareness of how all the external players, systems and agendas impact the client.

At different times, one may be attempting to give key perspectives to decision-makers, to hold a protected space for a child, or to be an agent of healing for damaged family relationships. There are intermittent windows of opportunity to have a healthy influence on a young client's life situation, but making the most of these depends on cultivating effective working alliances, monitoring one's own agendas and sustaining a flexible approach to how most usefully to define one's role in different instances.

The passive precept of not putting obstacles in front of the blind has also been interpreted as implying the active obligation of pointing out hidden dangers to one who is not aware of them (Leibowitz, 1986). Thus, it is relevant when trying to act from a position of integrity to attend carefully to the unacknowledged contextual variables.

Traditional ethical training of psychotherapists has emphasized giving care to the privacy of a client's inner world and doing painstaking assessment of her mental status, coping mechanisms and treatment needs. By contrast, the *Feminist Therapy Code of Ethics* (1987) states: "feminist therapists facilitate the understanding of interactive effects of the client's internal and external worlds." In a similar vein, Doherty (1995) emphasizes times when it is appropriate to use the lens of community rather than personal forces in viewing client difficulties. A microscopic view of the individual's attempts to manage pain often needs to be replaced with "a telescope" and its validation of the impediments imposed by forces in the society or community. Once more variations on a vision metaphor speak to the challenge of sustaining awareness of what may be relevant but hidden.

The metaphor of blindness has been explored by Ellyn Kaschak (1992) in her treatment of the Oedipus and Antigone myths. Oedipus cannot bear to "see" the patricidal and incestuous significance of his history, while Antigone puts her capacity for vision totally at her father/brother's disposal. The gaze of Oedipus is one that fragments and subsumes others as extensions of himself. Antigone, meanwhile, has to reclaim her eyes to see for herself. When a bureaucratic system reacts to child abuse, its strategies cannot but mirror the effects of the embedded race, class and gender oppression that are the source of many of the problems being addressed. Those of us attempting to be agents of healing within such systems have to grapple with our own blindness and stumbling blocks. We, too, become fragmented by the pain of our clients and the limiting, subsuming language of an agency. We, like Antigone, need to reclaim clarity of vision and awareness in order to sustain integrity where there is brokenness.

CASE EXAMPLES THAT HIGHLIGHT MORAL DECISION POINTS

Below I will be exploring instances of competing demands and judgment calls with the goal of delineating some common threads that would best guide decision-making using integrity as one's moral compass. In all these areas, using case examples, I hope to examine the press toward fragmentation and the hidden potential of acting from a position that supports some reclaiming of wholeness by attending to the contextual obstacles to healing. Just as talmudic cases extend applications of biblical injunctions, each of the cases below will extend the stumbling block/blindness metaphor.

RESPECTING A YOUNGSTER'S AGENDA

The story of Pablo (all names are pseudonyms) addresses the moral dilemma of managing confidentiality ethics when one's client's agenda conflicts with that of those responsible for his welfare. It also speaks to filling the often absent role of making a child's experience visible in the larger context.

Confidentiality. One has constantly to make decisions simply regarding what information is disclosed to whom. Legally one has a lot of latitude to share information "in the interests of the child," but the ethical challenge of defining an appropriate zone of privacy is more complex. In contrast to the classic procedures with adults of having release forms signed before having communications with any outside parties, I experienced encouragement in this multi-agency setting to use my own judgment. In many cases, sharing insights into a youngster's functioning is crucial to helping caregivers be sensitized to effective approaches in helping a child manage her distress. Many decisions regarding matters such as health management, family visitation and placement are made by social workers after consulting with therapists about a child's emotional functioning.

The moral dilemma here lies in how information can be used to further different agendas. In addition, a context of deprivation is not clearly acknowledged when describing a child's very fluid level of functioning. Like a cascade of mirrors, information can precipitate decisions that evoke further difficulties. I also gradually became more sensitive to the clinical implications of youngsters identifying their therapist as yet another component of an already untrustworthy system. By contrast, clients could be empowered by being informed and consulted about information exchange. When a client hears me transparently and respectfully share my concerns in her presence, it offers opportunity for more coherent self-reflection.

Case Example: Therapist as Advocate. Pablo was a large, tough-looking 13 year old who desperately wished to be re-united with his mother. His hurt at her difficulties in providing a stable environment was expressed in joining her anger at the "system" and acting out his despair by aggressive acts toward smaller boys and an oppositional style toward caregivers. He tested the therapeutic frame by transparent attempts to steal items from my office. In artwork he displayed dramatic tears of dripping paint. Despite his overtly impassive veneer, he passionately argued the value of being allowed to work on his educational deficits under his mother's care and sabotaged his progress in other settings. His social worker, appointed by the Department of Family and Children's Services, filled the role of evaluator with regard to placement planning. Past psychological evaluations of both Pablo and his mother had been ordered. His court appointed attorney (charged to represent his interests at a forthcoming mediation), requested feedback regarding his functioning and likely coping skills under different circumstances.

While I shared substantial concerns of other evaluators as to the feasibility of fulfilling Pablo's wishes and was legally authorized to share relevant information, I chose to position myself as his advocate rather than as an expert. Pablo had plenty of adults "objectively" identifying his problems and needs, but he had no source of validation for his rage, pain, confusion and disappointment. He had no model for appropriately arguing for his wishes or making sense of his losses. Thus, I stipulated that I would only talk about Pablo in his presence. Both with his attorney and later at a court mediation, I was able to speak about his anger so as to situate it within his experience of family rupture rather than as yet another symptom of his own or his family's dysfunction. However, acknowledging with Pablo his very limited capacity for tolerating frustration also allowed for integrating the importance of additional support into any placement or educational planning.

While respecting the voice of a client is an obvious guideline with adults, it is natural with minors to fall into the parental role of deciding what is good for the child. Ethically, this can often be justified, given the risks a youngster has limited capacity to evaluate. It was crucial, however, to Pablo's well-being to attend to the roles already being filled and select a moral position that avoided putting a stumbling block in the way of an already wounded person.

ENCOUNTERING PAIN

The case of Eva will explore the "expert" role and the client's "blindness" to how those in power would respond to and interpret her behaviors. I had to engage in a process of making visible the agendas of those impacting her life.

Recommendations. What guides one when called on to make recommendations that may significantly impact decisions made about clients' lives? Adolescents in "the system" are caught up in the contextual webs of their own family influences as well as of the dramas of limit-testing and identity formation that are worked out by challenging their institutional caregivers. Given the fluidity of their functioning, any expert opinion needs to stay loyal to underlying strengths and potential for learning, rather than to transient struggles and difficulties.

Case Example: Therapist as "Loyal" Expert. Eva, a 14 year old teen mother, was dealing with having been removed from her own mother, just as she was learning to be a parent herself. She was loyal to her family and struggled with the reports of neglect and addiction in the home. She was attentive to her infant, but was vulnerable to negative influences from peers and would resist following directions from staff about aspects of her parenting behavior. She, nevertheless, was positive and responsive to a parenting class that respectfully offered her healthy options. She would sometimes appear very composed, minimizing her problems, and other times voice feelings of anger and scornful impatience with authority figures that she perceived as attacking and judgmental. Therapy was voluntary, but she would be occasionally avoidant, making excuses rather than admitting her disinterest. As I named these contradictions and inquired into her true wishes, she slowly developed enough trust to seek my support in negotiating with authorities that were questioning her capacity to parent appropriately and be placed with her child. Her loyalty to her mother (who was perceived by social services as defensive and antagonistic) played a large part in the precariousness of her own situation.

Eva's loyalty to her family and infractions in the shelter were both characterized as signs of her being vulnerable to putting her child at risk. During the court hearing, I was able to describe her behaviors as part of her process of maturation. The authentic anger, fear, love for her child and pragmatism she displayed during this crisis contrasted with her earlier tendencies to gloss over the ways she would evade meeting expectations she disliked. As we faced together the realities of the child protective system, she found the courage to negotiate agreements that would put stressful demands on her but could allow her to remain with her child. The press toward fragmentation in this case lay in the legal distinctions between the interests of Eva and those of her baby. However, this youngster's capacity for identity formation and learning in the crucible of crisis was the unacknowledged component that needed to be voiced as much as any of the traditional risk factors.

It was extremely painful to face the possibility that Eva could lose her baby. It was not clear to me how far she would be able to progress in the maturation necessary to function well as a parent. My ethical obligation was to describe Eva fairly, but my moral obligation was to help Eva bring into her awareness not only her own processes of justifiable anger, avoidance and resentment, but also the realities of how those in power would interpret and respond to her behaviors. While I stayed loyal to her potential for growth, I had to convey authentically the reality of this crisis to her, in order for her to respond fully to it. This required acceptance on my part that the outcome could have been different and the moral courage to step out of my own investment in avoiding this loss. I could function as an expert for the court, describing her ongoing maturation process, but I also had to be an expert interpreting the "system's" reactions to the client. However, only her own capacity for integrating this knowledge as she displayed some maturation could determine the outcome.

TRUTH, LIES AND BUREAUCRACY

The story of Rita addresses fragmentation of the therapist, my "blind" spots and the questions I wish I'd asked regarding the embedded stumbling blocks of class, ethnic and gender oppression.

Truth and Complexity. A frequent dilemma when working with abused adolescents, their families and social workers, is the reality of multiple coexisting truths. Bureaucratic structures and strictures often exacerbate tendencies to present official helpers with convenient, but partial, versions of reality. Again we deal with what is only partly visible. How as an agent of healing can one support a more complex truth to evolve in a context of distrust, deception, and often oppression?

Case Example: Therapist as Interpreter. Rita is a bright and appealing Mexican-American 13 year old. She was perceived by the initial investigator as both a victim of sexual abuse by males in her family and as a rebellious adolescent, vulnerable to gang members and older men, who needed behavioral containment. This perception constituted a significant stumbling block, defining Rita as the problem rather than the problematic boundaries and lopsided gender arrangements within the family. For example, her grandmother, the family leader after her husband was disabled, was protective toward her uncle, the alleged perpetrator. Many family members felt anxious about this uncle who was viewed as a vulnerable, recovering alcoholic who had had "bad breaks." Her social worker believed that she and her mother with whom she had an extremely conflicted relationship should be treated independently. Relatives with whom she wished to be placed were viewed by the social worker (based on reports of her mother and an aunt) as a negative and prohibited influence.

My experience of Rita was of a secretive, angry, and inconsistent young woman with low self-esteem and incongruous emotions. Early in her stay at the shelter, when she had hopes of placement with relatives, she would state that she was "happy." However, during this time she was reacted to negatively by peers who objected to her patterns of stealing. Despite brief occasions on which she expressed wishes for reunification, she was frequently furious and rejecting toward the mother and aunt with whom she was permitted contact. She had always resented her mother for appearing to place male partners ahead of Rita. When she learned that she would be blocked from contact with the "forbidden" relatives, she felt bereft and thwarted, making despairing comments about her "messed-up family." Her behaviors and communications would then often generate further conflict among her relatives.

As I gathered more information from Rita and some adult relatives, a complex and unpleasant picture emerged of a constricting and confusing family. This was a superficially tight-knit family with immigrant grandparents and many aunts and uncles. The health problems of Rita's grandfather, the family patriarch, had paralyzed the family in many ways. Some of her mother's siblings had left the family home but were seen as disloyal. One aunt was disliked and envied (but depended upon) due to her financial success. Aunts and uncles that remained in the parental home suffered from mental illness, alcoholism, unemployment and feelings of failure within the U.S. culture. Rita's mother had worked successfully in a health occupation, but she had conceived children with a number of men, none of whom stayed to support his child. Thus, each pregnancy left her more financially and emotionally dependent on her family.

Rita embodied many of the conflicts within this family system, including the cultural conflicts between different expectations for how adult children individuate. Her mother had unsuccessfully left and then returned to the grandparents' home and Rita had been driven by the need to exit what appeared to be a stunting and overwhelming environment. Family members accused others of coaching her to make the allegations that had brought her into custody. At one point, one family member impersonated another to a social worker. These tendencies toward deception, recriminations and accusations may have revealed what could not be named, a process of "blindly" gesturing to where the pain lives. Rita, as she became more isolated from all members of the family, became more angry and despairing, more negative about therapy, and increasingly unmotivated in school.

The effect of Child Welfare involvement had further divided and fragmented the resources of this family. The grandmother's leadership was viewed as inappropriate; brothers were pitted against sisters; and Rita's mother felt betrayed by the one aunt that Rita trusted. There was reciprocal "blindness" as family members and "threatening" professionals reacted to, rather than interacting with, one another. By contrast, my goal was to frame Rita's difficulties as representing her need for the nurturance and modeling of *all* the women in her family together with their differing capacities to transcend oppressive forces in this culture. These included her grandmother's leadership and endurance, her mother's concern with her safety as well as her aunts' capacities for success in the work arena and in the task of generating an independently viable family. I wanted Rita to experience the possibility of being noticed and attended to without having to pit her family members against each other. These were very ambitious goals and I found only limited windows of opportunity to offer these unifying interpretations to key participants.

Bureaucratic obstacles accentuated these limitations. These included the difficulty I had in establishing a working relationship with the investigating social worker who had the power to prohibit and delay visitation with key relatives. In some ways, she and I, in our difficulty trusting each other's judgment and perceptions, mirrored the family's disconnection. Thus, the process of my offering a more integrated interpretation of how Rita could get more of her needs met in her family was a painful contrast to the existing discord and disconnection. It prematurely threatened Rita's coping mechanisms and generated antagonism and distrust toward me. I had to tolerate being experienced as yet another disappointing adult who could not mobilize the resources she needed.

In my struggle to make sense of the confusion and generate a better plan of action, I had missed the opportunity to converse with Rita about some key questions. I wish I had asked, "How does a woman get respect in this family?" and, "What sort of success is approved of in this family? How can parents protect children in a culture different to that of their own upbringing?" Male partners of Rita's mother appeared to have had greater power than her children to engage her attention. It would have been meaningful to explore with Rita ways to account for this by examining her mother's vulnerability to gender-based imbalances, rather than assuming that the imbalance arose because Rita had less intrinsic worth than her mother's boyfriends. Such a conversation might have made visible some contextual analysis of the class, gender and racial oppressions that had manifested in the conflict and anxiety that was permeating this family's functioning. Such awareness might have helped Rita to take a step beyond her reflexive reactions to the emotional deprivation and undue control that she perceived.

It takes a lot of time to acknowledge and process the impact of distrust, deception and oppression. However, by sharing my experience and filling an interpreter role with the new social worker on the case, I hoped to limit the damaging effects of intensified fragmentation in this family. The stumbling blocks included an overly narrow, judgmental definition of what elements in the family offered influences toward harm or health for Rita. My moral stance was to situate the solution within the family, rather than in further rupture, despite the great difficulty presented to those of us experiencing this family's anxiety, distrust and deception. Based on my analysis, plans were made to convene a Family Conference. (This is a format used by Social Services to try and enlist family strengths in the process of planning for the minor in custody.) Thus in small ways, I may have sown some seeds toward reclaiming some wholeness in both Rita and her family.

CONCLUSIONS

I have attempted to demonstrate that to function in a context of fragmentation from a position of supporting potential wholeness may be the most moral stance to uphold. This would suggest an imaginative stretch to respect all that is absent and unvoiced and the pragmatism to select the roles that most need to be filled. Thus, during times of crisis and dislocation, one can seek the windows of opportunity for healing, for reconnecting what has been severed, and for sowing the seeds for future strength despite a context of trauma and impairment.

For the person of the therapist, the stresses of this work illuminate the need to find wisdom from a moral and spiritual ground that transcends technique. One needs the integrity to encounter fully and tolerate the realities of damage and woundedness. This involves a commitment to sustaining clear vision, when it would be more tolerable to stay "blind." Staying conscious of all the stumbling blocks embedded in the Child Welfare system means resisting the pull to sleep and to fragmentation in one's therapeutic functioning. It requires an ongoing application of the question, "What needs to be made visible in this picture?"

Sometimes, the external obstacles emerging in and out of my awareness can seem insuperable. At these times I can only commit to persevering through the internal obstacles of numbness, burnout and helplessness. Staying human, responsive and engaged in the face of a context that contains overwhelming pain, limitation and hopelessness may be the toughest moral challenge of all.

REFERENCES

Abrams, J.Z. (1995). *The women of the Talmud*. Northvale, New Jersey: Jason Aronson.

Anderson, G. (1997). Introduction: Children, adolescents and their powerholders in therapy settings. *Women & Therapy, 20*(2), 1-6.

Doherty, W. (1995). Community considerations in psychotherapy. *The Responsive Community, 5*(2), 45-53.

Feminist Therapy Institute, Inc. (1987). *Feminist therapy code of ethics and ethical guidelines for feminist therapists*. Denver: Author.

Hubner, J., & Wolfson, J. (1996). *Somebody else's children: The courts, the kids, and the struggle to save America's troubled families*. New York: Three Rivers Press.

Kagan, S., & Schlosberg, S. (1989). *Families in perpetual crisis*. New York: W.W. Norton & Co.

Kaschak, E. (1992). *Engendered lives*. New York: Basic Books.

Leibowitz, N. (1986). Kedoshim 3–Misleading the blind. In *Studies in Vayikra Leviticus* (pp. 173-178). Israel: Ahva Press.

Schuchman, K.M. (1997). Feminist approaches to working with adolescents: Acknowledging competencies and developing alternative interventions. *Women & Therapy, 20*(2), 101-110.

Telushkin, J. (1991). Jewish ethics and basic beliefs, 255: "Do not put a stumbling block in front of a blind man" (Leviticus 19:14). In *Jewish literacy* (pp. 498-499). New York: William Morrow and Company.

In the Belly of the Beast: Morals, Ethics, and Feminist Psychotherapy with Women in Prison

Cindy M. Bruns
Teresa M. Lesko

SUMMARY. This paper addresses three primary moral and ethical issues faced by feminist therapists working with women in prison: (a) working in a racist and patriarchal institution, (b) conducting therapy in a setting that can be antithetical to the inherent vulnerability and the development of trust involved in the therapeutic relationship, and (c) the therapist's dual allegiance to the institution and the woman seeking therapy. A discussion of ways feminist therapists might morally and ethically work in a penal or other institutional system concludes this paper. *[Article copies available for a fee from The Haworth Document Delivery Service: 1-800-342-9678. E-mail address: getinfo@haworthpressinc.com]*

KEYWORDS. Women prisoners, morals, ethics, feminist therapy, incarceration

---

Cindy Bruns, MA, and Teresa Lesko, MA, are doctoral candidates at the California School of Professional Psychology at Alameda. They formerly worked as Psychological Trainees at the Women's Federal Correctional Institute at Dublin, CA.

Address correspondence to Cindy M. Bruns, MA, California School of Professional Psychology at Alameda, 1005 Atlantic Avenue, Alameda, CA 94501, or via the internet at cindymbruns@sprintmail.com.

The authors have contributed equally to the preparation of this article and are listed alphabetically. The authors would like to acknowledge and thank the following people: the women in prison with whom we worked, Cory Fitzpatrick, Amy Hutto, and Valory Mitchell.

[Haworth co-indexing entry note]: "In the Belly of the Beast: Morals, Ethics, and Feminist Psychotherapy with Women in Prison." Bruns, Cindy M., and Teresa M. Lesko. Co-published simultaneously in *Women & Therapy* (The Haworth Press, Inc.) Vol. 22, No. 2, 1999, pp. 69-85; and: *Beyond the Rule Book: Moral Issues and Dilemmas in the Practice of Psychotherapy* (eds: Ellyn Kaschak, and Marcia Hill) The Haworth Press, Inc., 1999, pp. 69-85. Single or multiple copies of this article are available for a fee from The Haworth Document Delivery Service [1-800-342-9678, 9:00 a.m. - 5:00 p.m. (EST). E-mail address: getinfo@haworthpressinc.com].

© 1999 by The Haworth Press, Inc. All rights reserved.

The image evoked by the word "inmate" is often that of the hardened, violent man with a long history within the judicial system and few attachments to society at large. In contrast to the vivid image of men in the penal system, women who are incarcerated have been an historically invisible population in the United States. Within the last decade and a half women inmates have begun to lose some of their invisibility, partially due to the dramatic rise in the number of women entering the penal system. Between 1980 and 1990 there has been a 256 percent increase in the number of women being incarcerated. Since 1986, there has been a 432 percent increase in the number of women imprisoned for drug offenses, compared to a 140 percent increase in the number of men being incarcerated for similar offenses (Watterson, 1996). In addition, the arrest rate for girls under the age of eighteen, while still behind that of boys, rose 82 percent from 1989 to 1994 (Sikes, 1997). As the invisibility of incarcerated women has decreased, some inquiry into the context of these women's lives and their particular psychosocial needs has begun. Incarcerated women tend to belong to multiple oppressed groups, the majority being women of color from lower SES backgrounds, who are often single mothers of minor children, have low educational achievement, and are usually under-employed (Watterson, 1996). In addition, childhood emotional, physical, and sexual abuse (Garcia Coll, Baker Miller, Fields, & Mathews, 1997); adulthood victimization (McClellan, Farabee, & Crouch, 1997); and severe emotional distress, psychological difficulties and substance abuse issues (Singer, Bussey, Song, & Lunghofer, 1995) are important contextual issues for incarcerated women. The elucidation of the relationship between trauma, its sequelea, and criminal activity in the lives of women (Lake, 1993) has led to the development of psychological treatment opportunities within many prison systems.

As therapists increasingly become involved in prison settings, they are faced with a unique set of ethical issues. Therapists must balance dual roles, for example, having both the institution and the inmate as clients, and being required to enforce correctional procedures in the therapeutic context. In addition, therapists must contend with the reality that there is often more need for services than can be provided by the psychology staff at any given institution and of working in a hierarchy that can impose constraints on service delivery. The ethical issues of practicing therapy in prisons from the classical perspective are complicated and require thoughtfulness on the part of the therapist.

When a feminist lens is applied to the prison system–a system that remains one of the archetypal "beasts" of patriarchal and racial oppression in U.S. society–and to the meaning of psychological distress and healing for women incarcerated in this system, the demands of morality and ethics interact in complex ways. The purpose of this paper is to elucidate many of the complexities faced by feminist therapists working with women who are incarcerated. Before beginning our discussion, however, a brief consideration of the distinction between ethics and morality is necessary. We will define ethics as explicit rules governing therapists' actions (*The American Heritage Dictionary*, 1983). These rules are exemplified by the codes adopted by the various professional organizations to which therapists and counselors belong. Ethical guidelines or rules tend to be behaviorally oriented, clearly explicated, and black and white. Morality will be defined as the larger principles of right and wrong (*The American Heritage Dictionary*, 1983) from which ethics are derived. Morality, while also governing therapists' decisions and behavior, tends to be more subject to individual differences, less agreed upon by organizations, and often influences how ethics are applied.

As the focus of this paper is on feminist therapy, the ethical and moral principles discussed will derive primarily from the Feminist Therapy Code of Ethics and its Preamble (Feminist Therapy Institute, 1990). The moral code that appears to undergird the ethical guidelines, as outlined in the Preamble, is comprised of the following principles: (a) the equal worth of all people, (b) a respect for, valuing of, and competence in understanding cultural diversity, (c) a recognition and valuing of the complex interaction of social and psychological factors in people's lives, (d) a commitment to reducing the effects of oppression, in all its forms, on the individual and societal level, and (e) an understanding of and responsibility for the use of power in therapy and society. From this perspective we will consider first the dilemma of working in a racist, patriarchal institution when one's principles and resultant ethics mandate cultural competency and a goal of impacting social change regarding all oppression. Next, the paradox of asking a client to participate in a relationship in which she will become vulnerable to a therapist who may be viewed as part of the various institutional oppressions (e.g., racism, classism, sexism, and homophobia) from which the client must protect herself will be explored. Finally, we will address the therapist's dual allegiance to the woman seeking help and to the institution. We will end our discussion by proposing ways feminist therapists might work with women who are incarcerated and, by extension, in other patriarchal institutions.

COMPLEXITIES

Working in a Racist/Patriarchal Institution

Feminist therapy can be particularly challenging in a setting that replicates multiple societal oppressions. The Feminist Therapy Code of Ethics Preamble states that "Feminism strives to create equal valuing of all people by recognizing and reducing the pervasive influences and insidious effects of patriarchy on people's lives" (Feminist Therapy Institute, 1990, p. 37). Complications arise when working in an institution that largely operates in polar opposition to one's principles and ethics.

The prison system is a microcosm of the patriarchal power system that not only emulates but surpasses the insidious oppression that exists in patriarchy. It is a power-over model that objectifies women. An incarcerated woman is often called by her first name or "Inmate _____" and defined by her crime and registration number. This objectification makes it easier to ignore the complexity of individual women's lives. It gives the namer, the institution or the one in power, the ability to define and name the other in such a way as to limit the acknowledgment of that person's contextual life. This power of naming and defining also enables the institution and its representatives to infantilize women who are incarcerated. Prison engenders dependency and creates frustration, while suggesting that dependency and actions of frustration are not viable ways of being in the world.

A feminist therapist has a mandate to be culturally aware and educated and to recognize when she or he cannot provide adequate services. As disproportionately more women of color are imprisoned (Watterson, 1996), it is imperative that more therapists who are also women of color are available to the prison population. Childs (1990), in writing about therapy in a community setting, raises the issue that "The likelihood that any Black woman will find a therapist who is also Black, a woman, and a feminist, is minuscule" (p. 195). While many institutions are recognizing the need for more diversity in their staffing, from an historical perspective the preponderance of staff has not been culturally diverse and outside referral is not a possibility. This provides more of an onus for any therapist working in prison, regardless of her culture, to become culturally competent with a wide variety of populations, specifically those who comprise the largest proportion of this population. This competency includes class and sexual orientation diversities.

Feminist therapists working within the prison, or any institutionalized system, may frequently find their moral principles at odds with the morality held by the institution and classical models of psychotherapy. Both systems locate the area of adjustment or problem in the individual in her relationship to society. It is the individual who must adjust to the norms of society even when these societal expectations are both culturally irrelevant and invalid in the individual's community (Childs, 1990). Certain sets of cultural norms can become pathologized while the dominant culture's expectations become the benchmark for health and legally sanctioned. Therapists may find themselves, particularly when conducting psychological assessments that may be utilized to evaluate clients for therapy, halfway houses, and treatment programs, at odds with the institutional morality. An assessor working from a feminist perspective may be able to adhere to the ethical guidelines by highlighting and considering issues of culturally specific norms, the influence of oppression on the person's behavior and world view, and in general creating a more complex view of the woman. At the same time, the assessor may find the assessment violating the moral principles of reducing oppression and working in culturally appropriate ways by using tests that often are not normed for the client's cultural group and in the end, judging the individual's ability not to reintegrate into her own cultural context, but to act in accordance with the laws, values, and norms of the dominant culture.

Making visible the racial oppression that is replicated in the prison from the society at large can be threatening to the institution. Society mandates that prisons keep those who are defined as threats securely locked away from the larger community. Viewing the woman who is currently incarcerated solely as a threat to society creates an additional layer of objectification. The context of her life is not seen and she is instead defined as the institution would define her. Given the racist and patriarchal nature of prison the dilemma faced by each feminist therapist is whether the feminist vision can be retained without being co-opted by the oppressive environment of the institution. Coping with this dilemma requires the therapist to engage in complex feminist analysis while resisting the pull to disregard the feminist lens.

The Paradox of Oppression and the Therapeutic Relationship

A feminist therapist working in a prison setting must remain cognizant of the woman's emotional vulnerability not only in therapy but also in the larger context of the client's life in prison. The prison setting is a perilous one for the exploration of self and context. At the same time, in comparison to their lives on the outside, incarcerated women may now have more support for their quest for self-understanding and change. Some women who are currently incarcerated may have attempted "to preserve a connection to the other by modeling external experiences of abuse and self-hate . . . (that) can create shame, rage, psychosomatic illness, anxiety, depression and destructive behaviors, including addictions and violence towards self and others" (Hertzberg, 1996, p. 133). For some clients entering therapy in a prison setting this may be the first time they have let themselves be vulnerable to the exploration of their emotional life and history. Others, who may have been punished for their expression of emotions, may be suspicious when met with this new acceptance of their process. When a client attempts to address these issues in a therapy session, she may feel unsafe re-entering the prison population with new and often painful discoveries. She will interact with not only other incarcerated women, but also with the correctional officers who may choose to exercise their power-over in any given situation. She may be confused, scared, and angry, which can be threatening emotions for others to encounter when she has been defined as a "criminal," a label that connotes aggression. She will be in the precarious position of addressing these emotions in a setting that is not conducive to, and often forbidding of, the expression of difficult emotions. The therapist must acknowledge both the danger and the safety of the woman's exploration as well as be cognizant of the power dynamics of the correctional institution and the therapeutic relationship.

Forming a therapeutic relationship in this context of power-over, fear, and wounding is a delicate process for both client and therapist. As Hertzberg (1996) notes

> Witnessing, empathizing, containing, and holding are essential aspects of the healing relationship. Many internal veils need to be removed, and a profound distrust of the other needs to be gradually healed. As socially conscious therapists, we must be aware of the intricacies of those 'protective' layers of invisibility, the fear, and toxic shame that can accompany this unveiling. (p. 143)

The intricacies of a client's invisibility in prison are complicated. In many therapy groups shame becomes a central focus, regardless of the chosen topic. Women describe it as an underlying dynamic that is continually reinforced in prison. How does the clinician explore shame with the client while acknowledging the clinician's part in a system that can reinforce this shame? Lerman and Porter (1990) list as one of the guidelines for feminist therapy that "the relationship between therapist and client should promote egalitarianism between the two and foster the client's self-determination and autonomy" (p. 5). Can egalitarianism be promoted in this setting? Is it inherently subversive to conduct feminist therapy in a prison?

A prerequisite of promoting self-determination is understanding that certain layers of invisibility may be required for a client to feel safe in prison. In examining these layers with the client it can be acknowledged that every person chooses to wear veils when needed. Implicit in this understanding is that people can also unveil as they become emotionally ready. Exploring the possibility of choice locates the agency with the client while acknowledging the potential dangers of the social context. Yet, promoting self-determination does not necessarily promote egalitarianism and it is questionable whether such an equalizing of power in the therapy relationship can be achieved in a prison or other institutional context. The specter of "therapist-as-correctional-officer" is a constant in the therapy relationship and blocks deeper levels of egalitarianism. Not only is this specter a threat to the therapeutic relationship, but it can be a threat to the basic moral principles of feminist therapy, especially the view of all human beings as having equal worth. The effects of institutionalized power on one's world view can be insidious and lead to hierarchical beliefs and actions by the most vigilant feminist.

The subversive nature of feminist therapy is the acknowledging and making visible within the therapy these complex roles and relationships that both clients and therapist must balance. In this process, a feminist therapist in a correctional setting must understand for her- or himself what is being meant by correctional. If we consider that moral–not just well-conducted–therapy considers the social construction of oppression, then we must carefully adhere to the ethical mandate to examine all aspects of our client's lives as well as our own. The power to define, de-contextualize, and re-contextualize criminals and corrections must be considered. McCarthy and her colleagues (1997) discuss that in the discourse about crime and violence there are "fundamental fables about the operation of power and the production of meaning and values in society." These fables are "moral re-evaluations" and our "collective tensions, crises, and fears" (p. 231). By projecting our collective tensions and fears on dis-empowered populations society can then have a moral reason for ignoring the context of their lives.

bell hooks (1984) notes that all people, even the least powerful, have some form of power. One description of power held by the weak is "the refusal to accept the definition of oneself that is put forward by the powerful" (Janeway, 1981, p. 167). Feminist therapists must strive to understand how each party in these complex relationships (the woman who is incarcerated, the institution, and the therapist) views and defines the other parties. In this process, the way in which morality and fear are owned and used by the powerful to define the less powerful in a narrow and de-contextualized way are made visible. In addition, the morals held by feminism that define people and relationships in layers of complexity and diversity also are made visible. The therapist can then aid the woman in both self- and other-definition that are broadening and complex while rejecting those definitions that are narrowing and limiting. In this process of creating complexity in a system that strives for parsimony, feminist therapy in prison becomes inherently subversive.

Dual Allegiance

Another complexity of conducting feminist therapy in a prison setting is the dual client relationship. The prison is the therapist's primary client and the incarcerated woman is a secondary client. The first and foremost consideration of prison officials is custody and security. For instance, in many institutions, if an inmate does not arrive for a scheduled appointment, she must be reported to a correctional officer who must then account for her absence. The therapeutic implications for this procedure are vast. One understanding of this reportability is that the incarcerated woman may not see the institution and the therapist as separate agents. Dual allegiance to the institution and the incarcerated woman may cause the therapist to act as an agent of the power-over model.

By acting in a correctional capacity the therapist may dis-empower and frustrate the client. The moral and therapeutic challenge becomes finding ways to use correctional procedures in ways that are empowering. One particularly difficult place to balance both needs arises when women are seen by the institution as behaving in ways that are not "under control." A woman's being "out of control" may arise out of dealing with difficult emotions in therapy. Balancing potential conflicting therapeutic goals becomes another ethical dilemma. A feminist clinician may consider all of these issues topics to discuss and work through with the client. By making these issues visible, the therapist can build rapport while using a potentially dis-empowering situation to empower the client.

Most ethical codes address the issue of dual relationships or allegiances in some manner, albeit often in vague terms, suggesting such relationships can be problematic for both client and therapist. For example, the Feminist Therapy Code of Ethics states that "A feminist therapist recognizes the complexity and conflicting priorities inherent in multiple or overlapping relationships" and is responsible for ensuring the client's safety from abuse (Feminist Therapy Institute, 1990, p. 38) and the American Psychological Association (APA) enjoins psychologists to "clarify the nature and direction of his or her responsibilities, keep all parties appropriately informed as matters develop, and resolve the situation in accordance with the Ethics Code" (APA, 1992, p. 1602).

Dual relationships frequently arise in a setting where the need for mental health services, both from the individual woman's and the prison's request, out-number the available staff. A therapist may be asked to perform a half-way house evaluation on a client she or he sees in therapy, thereby creating the dual role of therapist and expert evaluator. To whom does the therapist give her or his allegiance in this instance? To the primary client–the institution–and risk hurting the client and the therapy relationship if the evaluation goes poorly? To the secondary client–the woman–and risk sanctions by her superiors?

The resolution to this dilemma is not found in the ethical guidelines but in making a moral choice to serve the greater good. At times the choice may be to enter into the dual role, while at other times the choice may be to refuse the request for multiple roles. In making this choice, the health of the individual, institution, and society must be considered in complex relationship to one another and the therapist should, to the extent possible, make the decision process and the moral complexity of the situation as visible as possible to all those affected by the ultimate outcome.

PRACTICAL APPLICATIONS

Working in a patriarchal institutional setting presents feminist therapists with challenges and opportunities. As Laura Brown (1994) notes, " . . . it can be within mental health institutions that the subversive potentials of feminist therapy are most powerfully realized . . . and the possibilities for feminist capture of patriarchal institutions from within are increased" (p. 196). Practicing feminist therapy with women who are incarcerated requires active participation from the therapist on personal, therapeutic, institutional, and societal levels.

Feminist therapists make a commitment to examining their own oppressing biases and internalized "isms" as a matter of course. Part of this process often involves evaluating how one's place in society helps to keep one's role in oppression invisible and may lead to unconscious biases towards others. When working in an institutional setting which is an intensified microcosm of society, feminist therapists must be especially vigilant in their self-examination. For example, there can be subtle and not so subtle pressure from the system for incarcerated women to conform to essentially middle-class, white values and behavioral norms. There can be a pull for therapists to accept the institutional view as "normal" and "healthy" and view any deviation as pathological. More insidious is the thought that by encouraging a woman to act in prescribed ways, she may have an easier time of incarceration. Only through careful examination of one's beliefs, thoughts, behaviors, and biases can feminist therapists realize the ways institutional and personal forces interact and influence the practice of psychotherapy. Self-evaluation can be facilitated by the use of continuing education, supervision/consultation, personal therapy, and peer support.

Peer support is important, not only in confronting and overcoming oppressing biases, but also in coping with the stresses of working in a penal setting. Too often the feminist therapist works in isolation in patriarchal institutions where, although there may be opportunities to effect change, the social and political forces discussed in this paper remain deeply and firmly entrenched. The confluence of racism, sexism, homophobia, classism, and rigid, power-based hierarchies in "the belly of the beast" can begin to erode even the strongest feminist therapist. Support from other feminists who understand the intricacies of working within correctional systems, as well as the many issues facing incarcerated women, can be vitally important in maintaining a feminist ethic of care. When the demand for therapy so clearly outweighs what a therapist is able to supply, there can be a real desire to give more than one is able. A peer support group can also help therapists maintain a program of regular self-care, supporting an ethic of regular working hours, taking time for renewal and rest, and developing varied interests and relationships that can prevent "burn-out."

On the therapeutic level, much is required to conduct feminist therapy that honors both the ethical guidelines and the underlying moral principles. The bedrock of this work is the focus on informed consent. While informed consent is important in any setting, when working with women inside a system that exponentially increases the power differential between therapist and client, consent is infused with additional meanings. A feminist therapist has an ethical obligation to help the client understand that the therapist must play the dual role of healer and correctional staff. The implications of this duality need to be clearly articulated for the client, including the impact on confidentiality, the structure of therapy (e.g., issues related to attendance), and on the therapist-client relationship. Clients also must be informed of their rights as consumers and the methods of redress available within the system if they have a grievance against the therapist. It must be noted, however, that clients often do not see this as a viable option, given their place in the power structure. Clients may believe, and often rightly so, that their grievance will fall on deaf ears. In addition, therapists should make sure that clients understand what impact participating or not participating in therapy might have on their legal status. For example, clients often enter therapy with the expectation that participation will lead to a sentence reduction or look favorable to various correctional entities. Depending on the system in which a person is incarcerated and various other factors, this may or may not be true. An exploration of the client's beliefs and the realities of her situation should be part of making sure a treatment contract is entered into with full understanding. Finally, informed consent should include a discussion of the ways institutional matters may interfere with the negotiated treatment contract (e.g., the therapist missing a session because she was paged to an emergency; the client being unable to attend session because the facility is locked-down) and develop a plan with the client for handling these factors.

Feminist therapy with women who are incarcerated must, by definition, have at its center an awareness of issues of power, oppression, and diversity. Therapists hold the responsibility of managing the power differential between themselves and their clients (Feminist Therapy Institute, 1990). Included in this responsibility is the obligation to make visible factors leading to differential power in the therapy relationship and work from a stance of client empowerment. Empowering the client to understand the therapy relationship and see her choices, as well as helping her to take responsibility for her choices can increase the client's sense of power, especially if the institution is largely oriented towards correction rather than rehabilitation.

Making power dynamics visible is important for all clients, but may be especially important for women who are survivors of interpersonal trauma, since the likelihood of these women experiencing their incarceration as a revictimization is very high (Fromuth & Burkhart, 1992). Jan Heney and Connie M. Kristiansen (1997) suggest that

> . . . counselors should be cognizant of the dynamics of powerlessness and skilled in strategies that can help a survivor [or any client] move to a position of power from which she tries to control her own responses to external events rather than the events themselves. (p. 38)

This approach can also be used to help clients understand the connection between their incarceration and the structure of power in society (Phillips & Harm, 1997), and provide a vehicle for release planning. Groups can be a particularly effective way of working with issues of power and oppression, providing a powerful antidote, through connection with others, for the shame engendered by the patriarchy and racism.

The transmission of cultural knowledge and pride for members of oppressed groups is often overlooked or even discouraged by the dominant culture. Feminist therapists arguably have a moral obligation to bring to light diversity in a manner that values difference. The development of a positive cultural identity is important for the development of a positive self-image, increased self-efficacy, and reduced feelings of shame and isolation (e.g., Carter, 1991; Herbert, 1990). This growth can be facilitated through culturally specific groups and work with a therapist of similar cultural background who has developed a positive cultural identity. Given the sharp discrepancy between the percentage of women of color who are inmates and the percentage of women of color who are employed as therapists, white therapists bear an obligation to provide opportunities for incarcerated women to have contact with positive role models from their own cultures. Women of color may be brought in to speak with specific groups. More on-going contact can be facilitated through the hiring of women of color as staff and volunteer therapists. While many institutions may be supportive of ethnic diversity, deep-seated homophobia may prevent the inclusion of sexual orientation diversities. Feminist therapists may find themselves able to organize groups for women of color to explore specific cultures, but the organization of a group specifically for lesbians likely would meet with greater resistance from the administration.

Whether working in a group or individual setting, clinicians must be aware that clients may have issues about working with a therapist who is ethnically dissimilar. This awareness needs careful monitoring and balancing by the clinician. Although clients should be given the opportunity to explore their feelings, thoughts, fears, and biases, clients may not feel safe in discussing these areas in the context of incarceration. Discussions of this nature can be crucial to the therapeutic relationship and the client's healing, especially when the client does not have the option of working with a culturally similar therapist. The client's ability to engage safely in this discussion, however, must be carefully considered and her inability to do so should not be pathologized.

Finally, a client's cultural background; membership in multiple oppressed groups; her level of educational attainment; the quality and continuity of familial relationships; parenting concerns; and sexual, physical, and emotional abuse history are all layers of complexity that pattern her current life circumstances and level of emotional distress.

By holding this complexity, therapists will be more likely to help clients begin the process of reclaiming their "mother tongues" (Brown, 1994) and come to a deeper understanding of their current distress.

By accepting employment at a correctional institution, a therapist is taking the institution as a client and is responsible for facilitating the prison's goals as much as she is responsible to the individual client. Society has ostensibly charged prisons with enforcing safety, order, control, and the correction of what is viewed as "antisocial" behavior, or when this fails, keeping people permanently separated from society at large. The institution develops methods to obtain these goals and feminist therapists ethically cannot act completely outside of, or in total opposition to, these policies and procedures. Feminist therapists, however, can play an important subversive role by carrying out our mandate to "actively question(s) other therapeutic practices . . . and when possible, intervene(s) as early as appropriate or feasible . . . " (Feminist Therapy Institute, 1990, p. 40). By meeting institutional goals without reliance on punitive methods, the efficacy of feminist analysis and methods can be demonstrated to those in correctional power. The empowered inmate who possesses an awareness of power dynamics and the self-assurance to choose her response rather than react develops a greater sense of agency than the frustrated inmate who conforms out of fear of punishment. In addition, from the standpoint of the institution, she also becomes a significantly lower security risk. The more creatively a therapist can act within the confines of the system, the greater the potential there is for creating change, even if only in some small ways, at the institutional level.

Feminist therapy also carries with it an obligation to take an active role in the education of prison staff about issues relevant to incarcerated women. Staff need education in a variety of areas including: cultural sensitivity and competence; understanding of sexual, physical, and emotional abuse and its effects on psychosocial adjustment; and issues concerning sexual harassment. By increasing the correctional staff's knowledge and encouraging a more contextualized view of inmates, staff members may be empowered to begin to think creatively about "correction" and to act rather than react when incidents arise. In addition, education can bring to light heretofore invisible racist and misogynist institutional dynamics for individual staff and may encourage staff to challenge and hold one another more accountable for their attitudes and behaviors towards inmates. Similarly, feminist therapists must take an active role in policy creation and implementation. In the arena of psychological services, therapists can advocate for the development of gender specific programming that addresses issues of addiction, child and adulthood abuse, and parenting difficulties (Heney & Kristiansen, 1997; Phillips & Harm, 1997). They can also educate administrators on the importance of recruiting and hiring more women of color and bilingual persons in both therapeutic and correctional capacities. These examples carry powerful subversive potential as they simultaneously arise out of a feminist analysis and further institutional goals in less oppressive and more empowering ways.

This article has focused on the complex moral and ethical issues that arise for feminist therapists working in a correctional context. Although some of the issues raised are specific to prison contexts, most are applicable to feminists working in any racist and patriarchal institution. Inpatient and day treatment programs, elementary and secondary schools, and residential treatment programs are all examples of work settings that may remain firmly entrenched in the patriarchy. The clients served within these systems are often viewed reductionistically and judged against the norms of the dominant culture. Expressions of pain by an individual client may quickly become decontextualized and pathologized by those in power. The therapist, more often than not, must struggle with a dual allegiance to the individual and the institution. These dynamics may be intensified by the social context of a prison setting, as the Stanford Prison Experiment demonstrated 25 years ago (Haney, Banks, & Zimbardo, 1973), however, they cannot be disregarded in settings where the influence of the social context may be less readily apparent.

One final point must be made on the morality of working with incarcerated women–or any marginalized or oppressed group–from a feminist perspective. A foundational moral principle for feminist theory and therapy is a commitment to take a "proactive stance toward the eradication of oppression" and "recogniz(e) and reduc(e) the pervasive influences and insidious effects of patriarchy on people's lives" (Feminist Therapy Institute, 1990, pp. 37-38). Feminist therapists arguably have a moral obligation to work "in the belly of the beast" of the patriarchy and seek to subvert the system from within. Whether a therapist chooses to make working in such institutions a major or minor focus of her or his practice, oppressive settings should not be ruled out as co-opted by the patriarchy. Rather, these settings should be ruled in as potential places of employment or *pro bono* work.

Feminist therapists also have a moral obligation to *leave* their positions in institutionalized settings if the patriarchy begins to erode their morals and ethics. As discussed throughout this paper, the pull to disregard the feminist lens and the "burn-out" that can come from working against the system are very real threats to therapists in these settings. Just as damaging as the absence of feminist therapists from prisons, schools, inpatient hospitals, and residential programs is the presence of a feminist who has become part of the system against which she or he once worked. Making the choice to leave a system whose oppression had become too much to bear should not be construed as a failure on the therapist's part. Rather, the choice should be validated and supported as an inherently subversive act deriving from successfully monitoring the influence of the patriarchy in the person's life.

In summary, feminists working in settings characterized by patriarchal and racist oppression must continue to strive for creative solutions to the practical problems facing their individual and institutional clients with the goal of subversive healing ever before them. This leads to greater involvement on the societal level, working for change in laws and governmental policies affecting marginalized groups of people. Change and healing can be frightening in any situation. When the foundations of the patriarchy are threatened, however, the fear can become magnified into a backlash. Subversion at any level–individual, institutional, or societal–cannot be accomplished without careful consideration of the moral and ethical complexities of the situation. By working simultaneously inside and outside the system, feminist therapists are presented with a unique opportunity to "use(s) the master's tools to reforge, reshape, and transform each possibility for oppression into one of liberation and social change" (Brown, 1994, p. 199).

REFERENCES

American Heritage Dictionary, The (2nd ed.). (1983). New York: Dell Books.
American Psychological Association. (1992). Ethical principles of psychologists and code of conduct. *American Psychologist, 47*, 1597-1611.
Brown, L.S. (1994). *Subversive dialogues: Theory in feminist therapy.* New York: Basic Books.

Carter, R.T. (1991). Racial identity attitudes and psychological functioning. *Journal of Multicultural Counseling and Development, 19*, 105-114.

Childs, E. (1990). Therapy, feminist ethics, and the Community of Color with particular emphasis on the treatment of Black women. In H. Lerman & N. Porter (Eds.), *Feminist ethics in psychotherapy* (pp. 5-13). New York: Springer Publishing Company.

Feminist Therapy Institute, Inc. (1990). Feminist Therapy Institute Code of Ethics. In H. Lerman & N. Porter (Eds.), *Feminist ethics in psychotherapy* (pp. 37-40). New York: Springer Publishing Company.

Fromuth, M., & Burkhart, B. (1992). Recovery or recapitulation? An analysis of the impact of psychiatric hospitalization on the child sexual abuse survivor. *Women & Therapy, 12*, 81-95.

Garcia Coll, C., Baker Miller, J., Fields, J.P., & Mathews, B. (1997). The experiences of women in prison: Implications for services and prevention. *Women & Therapy, 20*, 11-28.

Haney, C., Banks, C. & Zimbardo, P. (1973). Interpersonal dynamics in a simulated prison. *International Journal of Criminology and Penology, 1(1)*, 69-97.

Heney, J., & Kristiansen, C.M. (1997). *Women & Therapy, 20*, 29-44.

Herbert, J.I. (1990). Integrating race and adult psychosocial development. *Journal of Organizational Behavior, 11*, 433-446.

Hertzberg, J. (1996). Internalizing power dynamics: The wounds and the healing. In M. Hill & E. Rothblum (Eds.), *Classism and feminist therapy* (pp. 129-148). New York: Harrington Park Press.

hooks, b. (1984). *Feminist theory from margin to center*. Boston, MA: South End Press.

Janeway, E. (1981). *Powers of the weak*. New York: Morrow Quill.

Lake, E.S. (1993). An exploration of the violent victim experiences of female offenders. *Violence and Victims, 8*, 41-51.

Lerman, H., & Porter, N. (1990). The contribution of feminism to ethics in psychotherapy. In H. Lerman & N. Porter (Eds.), *Feminist ethics in psychotherapy* (pp. 5-13). New York: Springer Publishing Company.

McCarthy, C., Rodriquez, A., Meecham, S., David, S., Wilson-Brown, C., Godina, H., Supryia, K., & Buendia, E. (1997). Race, suburban resentment, and the representation of the inner city in contemporary film and television. In M. Fine, L. Weis, L. Powell & L. Wong (Eds.), *Off white: Readings on race, power, and society* (pp. 229-241). New York: Routledge.

McClellan, D.S., Farabee, D., & Crouch, B.M. (1997). Early victimization, drug use, and criminality: A comparison of male and female prisoners. *Criminal Justice and Behavior, 24*, 455-476.

Phillips, S.D., & Harm, N.J. (1997). Women prisoners: A contextual framework. *Women & Therapy, 20*, 1-9.

Sikes, G. (1997). *8 ball chicks*. New York: Doubleday.

Singer, M.I., Bussey, J. Song, L.Y., & Lunghofer, L. (1995). The psychosocial issues of women serving time in jail. *Social Work, 40*, 103-113.

Watterson, K. (1996). *Women in prison: Inside the concrete womb (Rev. ed.)*. Boston, MA: Northeastern University Press.

The Personal, Professional and Political When Clients Have Disabilities

Rhoda Olkin

SUMMARY. When clients have disabilities, questions arise about boundaries, advocacy, and the interface between personal and political agendas. In *disability-affirmative therapy,* the clinician incurs responsibilities in multiple areas: understanding the minority model and its treatment implications; valuing disability culture; awareness of the distinction between disability and impairment; facility with discussions of values and disability dialectics; ability to integrate sociopolitical forces into treatment; facility with countertransference; ability to incorporate disability into the case formulation; staying within one's area of competence; working with disability within larger systems; understanding of disability in context; and valuing disability as part of diversity training, teaching, and research. *[Article copies available for a fee from The Haworth Document Delivery Service: 1-800-342-9678. E-mail address: getinfo@haworth pressinc.com]*

KEYWORDS. Disability, advocacy, disability-affirmative therapy, minority model

What is the boundary between client and therapist? How does therapy incorporate advocacy? How does it fuse personal and political

---

Rhoda Olkin, PhD, is Professor at the California School of Professional Psychology, Alameda, and the author of "Disability-Affirmative Therapy" (Guilford, in press).

Address correspondence to: Rhoda Olkin, 3000 Citrus Circle, Suite 120, Walnut Creek, CA 94598. Electronic mail may be sent to ROlkin@compuserve.com.

[Haworth co-indexing entry note]: "The Personal, Professional and Political When Clients Have Disabilities." Olkin, Rhoda. Co-published simultaneously in *Women & Therapy* (The Haworth Press, Inc.) Vol. 22, No. 2, 1999, pp. 87-103; and: *Beyond the Rule Book: Moral Issues and Dilemmas in the Practice of Psychotherapy* (eds: Ellyn Kaschak, and Marcia Hill) The Haworth Press, Inc., 1999, pp. 87-103. Single or multiple copies of this article are available for a fee from The Haworth Document Delivery Service [1-800-342-9678, 9:00 a.m. - 5:00 p.m. (EST). E-mail address: getinfo@haworthpressinc.com].

© 1999 by The Haworth Press, Inc. All rights reserved.

agendas? For some populations of consumers (women, and gays and lesbians), these questions are addressed in specific theories (feminist therapy, and gay-affirmative therapy). But what about clients with disabilities? How do the personal, professional and political arenas coexist or collide? What are the responsibilities of therapists treating clients with disabilities? What might constitute *disability-affirmative* therapy? What are the implications for psychologists of this model for training, teaching and research? The purpose of this paper is to address areas of responsibility for psychologists in their roles as clinicians, teachers, and researchers.

INTRODUCTION

Persons with disabilities are considered a minority group that has been disadvantaged in most areas of life: economically, politically, educationally, socially, and personally. As such they have been the subject of laws designed to protect their rights and interests, the most recent and far-reaching being the Americans with Disabilities Act (1990). Persons with disabilities share many features with other minority groups (see Olkin, in press), most notably prejudice, stigma, discrimination, and devaluation of the culture and norms of the minority, with concomitant pressure to assimilate to the majority culture.

Why should mental health professionals care about disability issues? First, because persons with disabilities constitute the largest minority group in America. Second, social justice cannot be achieved by advancing the cause of one group while continuing to subjugate another. Third, we can no longer assume that psychology is exempt, that disability issues are "special," as in "special education" and "special Olympics." Disability studies must join the mainstream in psychology, in part because, according to Linton (1990),

> some basic tenets of psychology run counter to core ideas in disability studies in at least three fundamental ways. First, psychology is responsible for the formulations and research conventions that cement the ideas of 'normal,' 'deviant,' 'abnormal,' and 'pathology' in place. . . . Second, psychology's emphasis on empiricism and its repudiation of standpoint theory or positionality as legitimate starting points for research work against the types of . . . analyses necessary to explicate the social construc-

tion of disability. . . . Third, . . . psychology primarily trains practitioners to intervene on the personal level rather than intervene to alter the environment. (p. 6)

Thus, we as individuals and collectively as members of a profession have a responsibility to challenge the assumptions about the place of disability issues in training, curricula, research, and therapy.

It should be clear that embracing a disability-affirmative model is a rejection of competing models, most notably rehabilitation psychology and the medical model, with their focus on impairment and de-emphasis on disability. When we reject the medicalization of disability, then the study of disability "contests the current academic division of labor in which the study of the phenomenon rests in the specialized applied fields . . . and the rest of the academy is largely exempt from meaningful inquiry into the subject of disability" (Linton, 1998, p. 2).

Before turning to issues of responsibility we first must define the population of "persons with disabilities." For this I borrow from Oliver (1996), who in turn is using a distinction now well established in the disabled community between "impairment" and "disability." *Impairment* refers to the physical, sensory, cognitive, or systemic condition which directly imposes a reduction in certain functions; the locus of difficulty resides in the person. *Disability* refers to those barriers and reductions in function imposed by the physical and psychosocial environment; the locus of difficulty resides in the sociopolitical environment. This paper addresses disability more than impairment, and the definition of people with disabilities has three elements: "(i) the presence of an impairment; (ii) the experience of externally imposed restrictions; and (iii) self-identification as a disabled person" (Oliver, 1996, p. 5).

Therapists incur several responsibilities when providing treatment for clients with disabilities. It was my original intent to present these responsibilities separately in three overlapping areas: the personal, the professional, and the political, but doing so would imply a distinction among the three. Yet it is a basic tenet of this paper that disability-affirmative therapy, like its cousins for women and gays and lesbians, rejects the artificial separation of these domains. Therefore what follows are points that span the three domains, moving roughly through the roles of clinician, teacher, and researcher.

The *personal* might be defined as those aspects of psychotherapeutic work which are inside the therapist–interior debates, cognitions, expectations, attributions, values and beliefs. The *professional* might be defined as those aspects of psychotherapeutic work which comprise the various roles and functions of the psychologist. These may include clinician, teacher, supervisor, consultant, and researcher. Less apparent but no less important are our functions as role models, activists, and advocates. The *political* might be defined as those aspects of work which carry implications and power beyond the individual(s) in treatment or training, and/or which encourage or empower clients or students to influence organizational, social, legal, or political change. It also incorporates the inverse direction: the effects of politics and oppression on the person.

The literature on culturally competent therapy typically refers to three domains: *awareness*, *skills*, and *knowledge*, and I would add *relationship*. Skills and knowledge may be more amenable to classroom training, while awareness and relationship may be more responsive to experience. How are awareness, skills, knowledge and relationship affected by disability issues? What are the areas that clinicians working with clients with disabilities should be aware of? What are the responsibilities of psychologists in their roles as teachers and researchers? What follows are fifteen disability-related areas to consider in our roles as clinicians, teachers, and researchers.

RESPONSIBILITIES

One: Disability as Minority. Psychologists should recognize and acknowledge that persons with disabilities constitute a minority group. Therapists generally are aware of their responsibilities for developing cultural competence, but unless we see persons with disabilities as a minority we will fail to apply our methods and process of increasing cultural competence to this group.

From this awareness of disability as minority, it follows that persons with disabilities are bicultural, living in both a disability minority world and an "able-ist" majority world. Thus, therapy with clients with disabilities by able-bodied therapists is cross-cultural therapy. The clinician must be open to the culture of disability, and flexible in ways of understanding the cross-cultural client. Without this, the clinician's perspective is narrowed through the lens of his or her own culture. "The clinician is likely to elicit information that he or she would be able to understand, and, thus, the clinician may be susceptible to finding only what has been sought" (Tseng & Streltzer, 1997, pp. 247-248). As with all cross-cultural therapy, it is not sufficient simply to append culturally relevant content to "regular" therapy. Culturally sensitive therapy requires development of a framework based on culture; culture is not an appendage but the body politic.

Two: Valuing Disability Culture. It is not useful to acknowledge disability as a minority group with its own culture if one then devalues that culture. Disability culture has its own history, language, humor, heros and devils. You cannot presume to know a person with a disability without knowing that person's culture. Language is a very important factor in the cohesion of a culture, and in establishing insider-outsider identification. Therapists should be aware of the power of language, and the nuances of language in a cultural context. For example, consider the words "disability," "handicap," "impairment," "dysfunction," "crippled," "wheelchair-bound," "normal," "spastic," "mentally retarded," "learning disabled." Which are acceptable? Which brand you as an outsider? Which are pejorative? It is not enough merely to be *told* this information; the process of discovering for oneself is a process of disability acculturation. We cannot escape the "fact that language and its use is not just a semantic issue; it is a political issue as well" (Oliver, 1996, p. 74).

Three: Models of Disability. Therapists should understand the three main models of disability–moral, medical and minority. The *moral model* holds that disability is a defect caused by moral lapse, sins, divine retribution, failure or a test of faith. It brings shame to the person with the disability and his or her family. The *medical model* asserts that the disability is a medical problem, a defect or failure of a body system denoting abnormality and pathology. It puts the person with the disability in the patient role, and the goals of treatment are cure or restoration to the greatest extent possible. In both of these models the locus of the impairment resides within the person, and those providing intervention are able-bodied. The *minority model* (also called the social model) views persons with disabilities as a disadvantaged and oppressed minority group that has been denied its civil rights. The emphasis is on the social conditions causing disability rather than on the impairment. Interventions include education, laws and increased enforcement of laws, greater economic equity, and increased physical and social access. It ascribes to a consumer model in which decisions about persons with disabilities are made by persons with disabilities. Therapists should be cognizant of the treatment and psychological implications of each model, be aware of their own model, and know how to help clients understand the client's own model. (For further discussion of the clinical implications of these models, and for methods to help clients understand their own models, see Olkin, in press.)

Four: Disability versus Impairment. Therapists should understand the distinction between impairment and disability, and allow the client to be the expert on his or her disability. However, the therapist should take responsibility for learning about impairments (Harsh, 1993). For example, a client who has long had multiple sclerosis should be able to expect that a therapist will familiarize him/herself with the basics of this disorder, including types, diagnostic process, prognosis, treatments, and typical effects on lifestyle and daily functioning. Then, the particulars of any individual with MS can be added to this framework. But persons with disabilities carry an enormous burden to continually educate others; therapy should not duplicate this burden, or it becomes another arena of oppression.

Five: Values. Disability raises the Large Questions in life. These include the value and quality of life, morality, normality and deviance, justice and equity, interdependence and responsibility, and mortality. Therapists must be prepared to ask and answer difficult philosophical and practical questions. Examples include: (a) How do we understand the suffering of children with leukemia? (b) How do we reconcile the idea that we would never want to live "like that," when people "like that" want to live? (c) How do we balance long-term goals with taking enjoyment of each day because you can never know what will happen? (d) Should I refuse to allow my child to attend a program that is physically unaccessible to me? (e) Should we teach clients who don't see themselves as part of a group that they are members of an oppressed minority? (f) What are the clinical implications of social oppression for those with developmental and/or cognitive impairments? (g) Given the dearth of empirical guidance on clinical treatment of persons with disabilities, what guides do we use in designing a treatment plan? (h) What are the short and long-term effects on clients when therapists incorporate notions of self-advocacy and political activism as part of treatment?

As we grapple with these questions we also hold beliefs about the therapy process, such as whether it should be problem- or growth-focused, what is a desirable length of treatment, what it is that changes as a result of therapy, the role of empirical research in our treatment, the place of minority issues in case formulations. These beliefs shape our work with *all* clients. The question here is whether these beliefs are based on an assumption of nondisability as the "normal" state, and whether we change these beliefs for clients with disabilities based on prejudices and stereotypes. We have a responsibility to make our values and assumptions and meta-cognitions about therapy known, at least to ourselves, and then to examine how we apply these to clients with and without disabilities.

Six: Dialectics. Disability issues encompass many dialectics, and enjoin us to formulate a coherent set of beliefs and values. In dialectical arguments, one end of the spectrum is always accorded a superior position over its opposite. For example, in the dialectics of researcher versus researched, empowerment versus oppression, normality versus deviance, the first term is the superior one. But for many of the dialectics posed by disability the term associated with disability (versus normality) is the lesser valued choice. Examples include dependence (versus independence), subjective (versus objective), absence (versus presence), and dysfunction (versus function). One of the dialectical tensions is between the notion of autonomy (with its attendant false sense of equity despite inequalities in power) versus autocracy (benevolence). What is missing is a model for deciding *with*, not *for*, persons with disabilities. However, we should note this as a goal; for example, the Americans with Disabilities Act requires an interactive process for deciding reasonable accommodations.

Disability issues challenge us to grapple with these dialectics, not as abstracts, but in everyday acts. For example, I am the faculty advisor to students with disabilities at a graduate professional school of psychology. Many students request that their meetings with me and their disability status be kept confidential. When I agree to do so I make their individual concerns and needs superordinate to those of the institution. In particular, I give up some power and opportunity for organizational multiculturalism–i.e., I cannot take the public and political actions at the institutional level that would in fact most improve the lives of students with disabilities at our campus. We all make personal choices that carry political weight. We cannot shy away from the implications of our actions related to disability issues by relegating disability to a subordinate position.

Seven: Sociopolitical. When working with a minority client sociopolitical issues join the therapy. The relationship of laws and court rulings to the everyday lives of minorities is tangible. For minorities, issues of oppression, discrimination, stigma, poverty, immigration, stereotyping, and powerlessness are not abstract concepts or only distally meaningful laws, but quotidian events, protections, and civil rights. These sociopolitical elements have effects on our institutions of teaching, research, and clinical practice. Therapists must be informed about the rights of persons with disabilities, and be prepared to help clients achieve their rights. For example, a client needs flexible leave over a six-month period for intensive treatment for Hodgkin's disease, or a student with a learning disability requests an essay rather than a multiple choice exam, or a supervisee with motor difficulties requests assistance with chart keeping. We may declare that we shouldn't give legal advice, but this maneuver won't absolve us of the responsibility for knowing basic laws and rights for persons with disabilities. (After all, we do advise clients about legal issues, such as actions that might be taken if a previous therapy involved a sexual relationship, or if a teenager may be seen in counseling without parental consent.)

However, therapists must not induce clients to be forever tilting at windmills. To paraphrase Thurgood Marshall, referring to his years as legal counsel to the NAACP, early in a war one must choose only those battles one can win. It is, unfortunately, still quite early in the war.

Psychologists should become informed about the social and political disability movement over the past thirty years. In so doing, one not only learns about disability as a culture, which is necessary for providing competent cross-cultural therapy, but also becomes able to integrate these sociopolitical forces into therapy, instruction, or research.

Eight: Countertransference. Therapists are human beings neither immune to nor above the negative socialization to disability. We must be open to honest self-examination of our own responses to clients with disabilities, including negative affect (e.g., anxiety or repulsion) and cognitions (e.g., "I would never live like that"). We must be able to accept clients' intense emotions, such as grief, terror, rage, physical and emotional pain. Persons with disabilities live in the shadow of uncertainty: "Will my impairment get worse?" "Will I have enough energy to do that task tonight?" "Will the building be accessible?" "Will there be handicapped parking?" Disability requires a high tolerance for this uncertainty, and also for pain, powerlessness, discrimination and oppression. It is easy for therapists to avoid these issues by downplaying their salience or impact. Conversely the client may be viewed as heroic for withstanding the onslaught of physical and emotional demands of disability. As Wright (1983) explains, people think *You are disabled, therefore you must be suffering. If, in light of overwhelming evidence, I see that you are not suffering, it must be because you are superhuman, heroic.* None of these stances (suffering versus heroism, downplaying of the extent of stigma and oppression) is realistic or helpful to the client.

Disability forces us to recognize that the world is not just, that lightning can strike anyone, and thus we face our own vulnerabilities. Therefore, in addition to tolerating affect in our clients, we must tolerate in ourselves the strong emotional reactions generated by disability. We may experience aversion, repulsion, horror, terror, sadness. Even those of us with disabilities are likely to hold prejudices and stereotypes against other types of disabilities. There is a powerful hierarchy of acceptability of disabilities (Olkin & Howson, 1994), and we are not immune from discrimination against those with less acceptable disabilities. Our countertransference issues are likely to include a bias against deviance, defenses against the hopelessness of a disability with no "cure," and feelings of incompetence. We might bolster our professional esteem by convincing ourselves that we are good generalist therapists, and therefore can utilize our skills with most populations of clients. It takes the sturdy among us to face these feelings and beliefs head on. There probably is no remedy for "able-ism" more powerful than immersing oneself in disability culture, viewing over a period of time persons with disabilities in "normal" functional roles and social interactions. For example, when my class attended a three-day workshop on parents with disabilities, at which more than half of the attendees were professionals with disabilities, one student commented that she felt "transformed." This is possible only when we encounter the "other" on an equal basis, not as professional and client, helper and helpee.

Nine: Case Formulation. Disability is often seen as a *central characteristic*, one that defines the person and overshadows other attributes. When a characteristic is central it carries with it a set of other assumed characteristics that may or may not be accurate. Disability is a central characteristic. When other attributes are unknown its role is profound in impression formation. Therapists must strive to see the disability as one aspect, but not necessarily the defining aspect, of a human being who comprises many facets. Furthermore, disability should not be decontextualized–it is not a trait floating around on its own, but rather occurs in the context of a person with other attributes; there is always the disability *and* _____ (gender, age, ethnicity, sexual orientation, etc.). We cannot understand the experience of disability for any one person outside of the context of the ands.

To assure that disability is playing neither an excessive nor overly minuscule role in case formulation, we should develop cultural competence in the skill of hypothesis-generation at both etic and emic levels, with concomitant openness to disconfirming data. Presence of an impairment, no matter how severe, does not mean it is the presenting problem, or even a major part of the presenting problem. (As hard as it is for able-bodied people to believe, disability is not necessarily the lens through which the person with a disability views the world.) We must guard against the possibility of the presence of impairment overshadowing other diagnoses (Reiss, Levitan, & Szyszko, 1982).

Ten: Competence. Therapists are ethically bound not to practice outside their areas of competence. As such, they have a responsibility to increase knowledge, skills, and proficiencies such that they can formulate cases and develop appropriate intervention strategies for clients with disabilities. Saying that one doesn't treat clients with disabilities is rather like saying one doesn't treat depression–you never know where in the therapy the issue will arise, and the ability to provide treatment for this problem is fundamental to our work.

Therapists must be knowledgeable about how theory and techniques are culture-bound, and about the effects of these on other cultural groups. There must be a basic understanding of how the world view of clients might be partially shaped by disability experience. And the therapist's understanding must include issues of power, submission, subordination, alienation, anger, and wariness. If the therapist is able-bodied, s/he must be familiar with insider/outsider considerations. And it is vital that psychologists understand the effects of specific types of disabilities on standardized tests and assessments, and not use tests normed on the able-bodied to derive overly pathologizing assessments of persons with disabilities.

Eleven: Systems. Disability, like feminist theory, is about "the phenomenology of connection" (Brown, 1990, p. 227). Therapists should (a) recognize that therapy is not just about the client with a disability, but about broader systems, and (b) know how to incorporate broader systems into the treatment. At the very least therapy should be able to include the family, as disabilities happen not just to persons but to families.

Therapists may have to incorporate even broader systems into the treatment. These systems may include personal attendants, other types of caregivers, the medical service delivery system, orthotists, state departments of rehabilitation, etc. Additionally, the family will interact frequently and often in times of great stress with these service delivery systems. It is important to recognize that persons with disabilities and their families generally have a full and often negative history with these systems. It falls to the therapist's responsibility to be able to integrate these systems, with their disparate cultures and goals, into a cohesive treatment approach.

There are even bigger systems, such as the American Psychological Association accreditation process for programs and internships, ethics codes, institutional and organizational systems, and funding sources. Not all psychologists see their work as incorporating these larger systems. But it is hard to work with families or students with disabilities without feeling the direct effects of such systems on the lives of persons with disabilities. For example, in our recent APA-accreditation site visit I raised the question of who holds the responsibility of providing reasonable accommodations to practica students and interns with disabilities. Because this question has been largely unaddressed, such students too easily fall through the cracks of service provision.

Twelve: Disability and [Blank]? We have a responsibility not to define away "minority status" by asserting that all people are different, or dismissing the minority experience by stating that all people have "handicaps" of one kind or another, and we must learn about each client individually. We must not trivialize the minority experiences of prejudice, stigma, discrimination, and devaluation. Nor should we do among ourselves what others do to us, by considering only one minority status at a time while excluding others. For example, the organized disabled community is mostly Caucasian. At the disability conferences I've attended the blacks are from Africa, and African-Americans and other ethnic minorities from the U.S. are notably scarce. Some attendees also complain that we duplicate in our organizational structure the hierarchy of acceptability of disabilities, and exclusion of inconvenient disabilities.

Thirteen: Disability as Part of Diversity. The role of disability in diversity training should not be underplayed. We must bear the responsibility of ensuring that disability topics are richly incorporated into such training, and not wait for persons with disabilities to force the issue. There probably never will be a sufficient critical mass of faculty or students with disabilities to demand a place for disability issues in the curriculum. Most programs have one or no students with disabilities at any one time.

Many training programs and clinical training programs have made the choice to focus diversity training on race. The idea is that racism is so pervasive that we must start there before moving on to other minorities. However, precisely because racism is so pervasive, this issue will never be "finished." However, whenever people discuss opening up the "minority" arena to other groups (e.g., gays and lesbians, persons with disabilities, the elderly), there is a fear that this more broadly-defined target group will be used to avoid or divert attention away from the difficult issues of racism. This is a real concern. However, if the door that is opened a crack for race is not held open long enough to let disability squeeze through, disability will never become the subject of attention. As difficult as issues of race and racism are, the issues related to disability are also difficult. We must pay attention to disability issues, take the initiative, and do it now. We can mingle minorities in our training. As one study indicates (Bluestone, Stokes, & Kuba, 1996),

> multicultural training and training related to other areas of diversity can coexist. . . . [c]ourses with the highest ratings for coverage of multicultural content also obtained high ratings across the remaining diversity dimensions . . . these findings . . . may potentially quell the fear . . . that focusing on a broader range of diversity issues will detract from multicultural competence within programs. (p. 398)

Fourteen: Teaching. Teaching is more than the imparting of knowledge:

> An implicit assumption in much educational research is that teaching centers around the transmission of information and the

cultivation of certain cognitive skills. Yet we would argue that many transformations of central concern to teachers generally, and to teachers of psychology in particular, fall in the realm of belief and attitude change. That is, teaching is at a fundamental level a process of persuasion. (Friedrich & Douglass, 1998, p. 549)

Disability studies is about persuasion, and is both an academic pursuit and a political act. It is owned by persons with disabilities. It asserts that the study of disability is mainstream: "Disability studies is no more an optional 'additive' to the liberal arts than is the study of gender or race" (Berube, 1998, p. *x*). Why do people on the privileged side of race, gender, and/or sexual orientation support laws and movements and studies that may never affect them directly, but view disability studies, which may one day pertain directly to them, as special? "The field of disability studies is even more marginal in the academic culture than disabled people are in the civic culture" (Linton, 1998, p. 3).

The modal number of courses on disability in APA-accredited clinical and counseling programs is zero (Olkin & Paquette, unpublished manuscript). What is the meaning of this? "The curriculum is a manifest expression of the cultural values just as laws are manifest expressions of what a society deems to be right or wrong behavior" (Kliebard, as cited in Linton, 1998, p. 1). Yet disability studies would seem to be a logical and intrinsic part of clinical psychology training: "Disability studies takes of its subject matter not simply the variations that exist in human behavior, appearance, functioning, sensory acuity, and cognitive processing but, more crucially, the meaning we make of those variations" (Linton, 1998, p. 2). By omitting disability studies from training programs, our inaction is tantamount to a political stance that reinforces the marginalization of people with disabilities. "Scholars and activists have demonstrated that disability is socially constructed to serve certain ends, but now it behooves us to demonstrate how knowledge about disability is socially produced to uphold existing practices" (Linton, 1998, p. 4). If we hope to increase the representation of persons with disabilities in the profession, then as mentors and guides for a new generation of persons with disabilities we must show that we have set a place for them at the table.

Fifteen: Research. Regarding research, we have a responsibility to understand the different models and paradigms of research on disability (Olkin, 1997) and to be aware of how research is used and misused against those it studies. We should include persons with disabilities in all normative samples. Research is no longer needed that compares "disabled" and "normal" populations. And as Yuker (1994) declared, we should "stop studying the presumably horrible negative effects of a child with a disability on parents and siblings" (p. 12).

The "social relations of research production . . . are built upon a firm distinction between the researcher and the researched" (Oliver, 1992, p. 102). Traditionally able-bodied persons have been the researchers, and persons with disabilities have been the researched. This has allowed a disconnection between the authentic voices of persons with disabilities and the professional and academic empirical literature about such persons. We must bridge that gap by allowing persons with disabilities to be the researchers and the researched, and by including voices of disability in research seemingly not about disability.

CLINICAL EXAMPLE
AND A CHALLENGE TO THERAPISTS

The ideas in this paper may seem obvious and prosaic. But if they were easy to implement, people with disabilities would not experience such pervasive discrimination, and I would not hear such horror stories from clients with disabilities about what their previous therapists said to them. Before we declare that *we* are not like *that*, let me issue you a challenge to take responsibility for an assessment of your own values, beliefs, cognitions, perspectives and behaviors as a therapist who might see clients with disabilities. Read the following clinical example, then respond to the questions that follow.

> Sally is a Latina married woman in her early thirties with two young children. She had polio as a child in Mexico. As a result of the polio one leg is about two inches shorter than the other, her back is severely curved in a hunched position, and her arms are smaller than expected and of limited utility. In recent years she has experienced an increase in pain, fatigue, and muscle weakness (the hallmarks of Post-Polio Syndrome).
>
> Sally works in administration for a school district, but feels that she is "hidden in the back room." Her face is of average

prettiness, but her hair is cut in an unflattering short style because it is difficult for her to wash, brush, or style her hair. She mostly wears pantsuits to hide her leg length and girth differential, and the brace on one leg. She doesn't wear scarves or jewelry because they are too hard for her to put on. Her appearance is not particularly flattering. She has interviewed for other positions without success, and feels that her disability, particularly her deformed look, has prevented her from getting job offers. Her marriage is stable but unhappy, and she has frequent thoughts of leaving. However, she thinks she cannot leave the marriage because she depends on her husband for physical care and housekeeping tasks, could not support herself and her children on her salary alone, and because she is convinced that no other man would date her, so she would be alone for the rest of her life. She is worried about the effects of aging on her disability, and her long-term survivability. She presents in therapy as someone who is ugly, angry, and hopeless.

Questions

1. Sally wants to apply to the clinical psychology program where you are on the faculty. What might be your reasons to admit her and not to admit her?
2. How willing would you be to work with Sally as a client? In what ways do you think you are competent to do so, and what are the areas in which you do not feel competent?
3. Make a list of what you believe are all of the presenting problems, then list them in order of priority in your opinion, and then in what you think would be Sally's opinion. How are the lists the same or different?
4. What role has discrimination, prejudice, and oppression played in Sally's current situation? What is the relative contribution of her ethnicity and disability status to these factors?
5. What is your case formulation, and what are the roles of disability, ethnicity, and gender in this formulation?
6. How receptive do you think Sally will be to therapy with you? What do you imagine to be the areas of alliance? of resistance? of countertransference?

7. Are there any ideas in this paper that have persuaded you to see this case differently than you might have before you read it? Why or why not?

CONCLUSIONS

Should persons who are members of a minority group, whether based on ethnicity, sexual orientation, gender, or disability status, be offered treatment that affirms their minority status as a positive and valued attribute? As it turns out, this is the easier question. The harder questions arise after we answer that first question "Yes, of course." It is in the implementation of minority-affirmative therapy that the complexities and conflicts are manifest, and where countertransference feelings, unspoken values, cherished beliefs, and therapeutic persuasions are most challenged.

On the final page of the novel "The Fixer" (Malamud, 1966), Yakov, a hapless Jew in Czarist Russia, having undergone a systematic stripping of his liberty and dignity, thinks, "There's no such thing as an unpolitical man, especially a Jew. You can't be one without the other, that's clear enough. You can't sit still and see yourself destroyed." For minorities in America, there is no such thing as an unpolitical therapy.

REFERENCES

The Americans with Disabilities Act of 1990, 101,42 U.S.C., 12111; 12112.
Berube, M. (1998). Foreword: Pressing the claim. In S. Linton, *Claiming disability: Knowledge and identity*, pp. vii-xi. New York: New York University Press.
Bluestone, H.H., Stokes, A., & Kuba, S.A. (1996). Toward an integrated program design: Evaluating the status of diversity training in a graduate school curriculum. *Professional Psychology: Research and Practice, 27*(4), 394-400.
Brown, L. (1990). What female therapists have in common. In D. Cantor (Ed.), *Women as therapists* (chapter 14; pp. 227-242). New York: Springer.
Friedrich, J., & Douglass, D. (1998). Ethics and the persuasive enterprise of teaching psychology. *American Psychologist, 53*(5), 449-462.
Harsh, M. (1993). Women who are visually impaired or blind as psychotherapy clients: A personal and professional perspective. *Women & Therapy, 14*, 55-64.
Linton, S. (1998). *Claiming disability: Knowledge and identity*. New York: New York University Press.
Malamud, B. (1966). *The Fixer*. New York: Farrar, Straus & Giroux.

Oliver, M. (1992). Changing the social relations of research production. *Disability, Handicap, & Society,* 7(2), 101-114.

Oliver, M. (1996). *Understanding disability: From theory to practice.* New York: St. Martin's Press.

Olkin, R. (1997). Human rights of children with disabilities. *Women & Therapy,* 20(2), 29-42.

Olkin, R. (Spring, 1997). Five models of research on disability: Shifting the paradigm from pathology to policy. *Newsletter of the American Family Therapy Academy, #67,* 27-32.

Olkin, R. (In press). *Disability-affirmative therapy: An approach based on family systems and the minority model of disability.* New York: Guilford Press.

Olkin, R., & Howson, L. (1994). Attitudes toward and images of physical disability. *Journal of Social Behavior and Personality,* 9(5), 81-96.

Olkin, R., & Paquette, T.J. (1991). *The role of disability in diversity: A survey of APA-accredited clinical and counseling programs.* Unpublished manuscript.

Reiss, S., Levitan, G., & Szyszko, J. (1982). Emotional disturbance and mental retardation: Diagnostic overshadowing. *American Journal of Mental Deficiency,* 86(6), 567-574.

Tseng, W., & Streltzer, J. (Eds.) (1997). *Culture and psychopathology: A guide to clinical assessment.* New York: Brunner/Mazel.

Wright, B.A. (1983). *Physical disability: A psychosocial approach* (2nd ed.). New York: Harper & Row.

Yuker, H.E. (1994). Variables that influence attitudes toward people with disabilities: Conclusions from the data. *Journal of Social Behavior and Personality,* 9(5), 3-22.

Morality and Responsibility: Necessary Components of Feminist Therapy

Kayla Miriyam Weiner

SUMMARY. This paper addresses the need to (1) support the personal moral belief system that each individual brings into the therapy room, (2) help the individual nourish and develop her/his own system of being in the world that is congruent with her/his sense of right, and (3) incorporate a sense of morality and responsibility into the therapy process when it is lacking. Case studies will present the dilemmas that two women faced concerning the conflict they experienced between their responsibility to their families and their responsibility to themselves. *[Article copies available for a fee from The Haworth Document Delivery Service: 1-800-342-9678. E-mail address: getinfo@haworthpressinc.com]*

KEYWORDS. Morality, therapy, responsibility, psychology

There is a need to find a word, the right word, to describe something that has been missing from the therapeutic analysis, process and relationship as generally taught and practiced in the United States. The component often left out of the therapy room is that part of the individ-

---

Kayla Weiner, PhD (Clinical Psychology), is in independent practice in Seattle, WA, and is author of several articles about the theory and practice of feminist therapy and co-editor of *Jewish women speak out: Expanding the boundaries of psychology*, a book composed of a series of articles about the psychology of Jewish women. Her joy is filling her free time with friends, pets, gardening and travel.

Address correspondence to: Kayla Weiner, PhD, Pioneer Building, 600 First Avenue, Suite 530, Seattle, WA 98104. (e-mail: activist@foxintemet.net)

[Haworth co-indexing entry note]: "Morality and Responsibility: Necessary Components of Feminist Therapy." Weiner, Kayla Miriyam. Co-published simultaneously in *Women & Therapy* (The Haworth Press, Inc.) Vol. 22, No. 2, 1999, pp. 105-115; and: *Beyond the Rule Book: Moral Issues and Dilemmas in the Practice of Psychotherapy* (eds: Ellyn Kaschak, and Marcia Hill) The Haworth Press, Inc., 1999, pp. 105-115. Single or multiple copies of this article are available for a fee from The Haworth Document Delivery Service [1-800-342-9678, 9:00 a.m. - 5:00 p.m. (EST). E-mail address: getinfo@haworthpressinc.com].

© 1999 by The Haworth Press, Inc. All rights reserved.

ual which she holds to be sacred; that which is a guiding force in her being; that which helps her decide how to relate to others. The behaviors of the individual are such not because there is a law or someone else controlling them, but rather because the person has come to believe it is how she must lead her life. It is an internal regulator that lets one know the difference between right and wrong; that allows one to feel at peace with oneself.

Often religions give individuals the structure for this, but the word religion has too many connotations to be useful. The word spirituality has become the current word of choice that is intended to suggest one believes in, and has some relationship with, a guiding force of another dimension. The term spirituality has become a cliché and therefore also is not useful. I wish to introduce the concept of "morality of the soul." I am using the word soul to describe that part of the individual that is both conscience and "heart" combined; a personal belief system that gives purpose and meaning to an individual.

A plethora of material exists on the subjects of ethics and morality, but it is very confusing as definitions are inconsistent. Many sources discuss rules or guidelines for dealing with specific situations, such as the use of certain medications (Fallon, Liebowitz, Hollander & Schneir, 1990), research with the ill (Brom & Witztum, 1995; Frank, 1992), or group and family therapies (Lakin, 1994), all under the rubric of morality when they are actually talking of ethics of practice. Some works even attempt to define and theorize the development of morality in individuals and groups (Gibbs, 1993; Kitwood, 1990; Kurtines & Gewirtz, 1991; Lee, 1997; Madanes, 1997; Mullan, 1991) without clearly defining the difference between ethics and morality.

When I speak of ethics I am referring to the rules that govern human behavior, that allow society to function constructively and protect human relationships. Ethics are external rules, are relatively rational and linear, yet are contextual and mutable. Morality has to do with believing in the "rightness" of things. Morality is an individual's integration of ethics into the soul. Morals are inner drivings and, although abstract, are immutable (Hirsh, 1976). They arise from conscience and are psychological rather than physical or tangible. One acts morally because of an internal sense or firm conviction of what is right, rather than upon actual evidence or demonstration.

I would suggest that the Ten Commandments could be viewed as ethical law and the Golden Rule considered moral principle. There are laws forbidding one to murder another. Yet, if one is being attacked, and the only way to survive is to kill the attacker, then this (ethical) law is abandoned in the interest of survival. However, if one is in a situation where a life is not threatened, yet an enemy could be killed, moral principles would prevent the killing. To kill would be a betrayal of one's moral code and a denial of the soul. Prilleltensky (1996) suggests that in a psychology concerned with oppression and liberation, human values inform conceptions of the good life and the society, whereas moral principles help resolve conflict among competing values.

To help explain this concept with a secular example, I turn to the laws against speeding which are designed to protect all citizens and keep people safe. If one is seriously ill one would be justified in speeding to get help. However, one could not run down another person who happened to get in the way. The rules of speeding might be compared to ethical laws while respect for another person has to do with morality. Ethics tell us what behaviors are allowed and what are not allowed. Morality tells us what we believe we should or should not do based on respectful treatment of all humans and a desire for constructive relationships.

INDIVIDUAL AND SOCIAL INTERESTS

Women have been oppressed for years and molded into a system whereby their/our needs were and are made secondary to the needs of everyone else, in their families in particular, and society in general. In contrast, psychotherapy tends to fosters a narcissistic stance for therapists and clients whereby women are encouraged to focus on their personal needs. This mindset has sometimes supported actions by an individual at the expense of, or at best, indifference to, the needs of others. When a woman is reluctant to assert her needs she may feel shame because she/we live in a society that generally has a "me first" attitude. This shame may be compounded by the implied or overt position of the feminist therapist who serves as a role model for her women clients.

Feminist therapy has been vocal in advocating for the self care of an individual woman and, for instance, would generally encourage a woman to leave an abusive situation. However, if the woman does not leave, some therapists find it difficult to understand and are not able to comprehend the caring that may exist in the relationship. The ethical belief system and internal moral code of the individual, as well as the known and unknown implications for all members of her family, may make a break difficult and sometimes impossible. It is often even more difficult for a woman to leave when there is no obvious abuse; there are moral and spiritual considerations that may prevent her from declaring her complete independence.

Lemas (1997) notes that Freud's interest in both research and therapy, science and healing, expressed itself in a methodology that placed the questions of morality to one side. He suggests that a moral vacuum was developed that has undermined the therapist's ability to confront important issues directly and honestly. Nicholas (1993) noted the difficulty therapists seem to have discussing personal morality. She (1994) believes psychotherapy frequently strives for moral neutrality; i.e., where there is no discussion of the individual virtues of altruism, responsibility, justice, egalitarianism and honesty. She believes that neglecting morality can actually stymie the successful achievement of a client's stated goals. Erickson (1997) goes so far as to propose that psychotherapy as it is often practiced can confuse one's sense of morality and can blur moral distinctions by accepting shared social assumptions, by adhering to the medical model and by emphasizing individual goals. London (1986) examines the questions of whether a therapist's job is to help change the client's behavior to match prevailing moral beliefs or change the moral beliefs of an individual so that a troublesome behavior becomes acceptable and is no longer painful to the person.

Doherty (1995) argues that therapists since the time of Freud have overemphasized individual self-interest, giving short shrift to family and community responsibility. He clearly calls for the inclusion of moral discourse in the practice of psychotherapy and the cultivation in therapists of the virtues and skills needed to be moral consultants to their clients. He argues " . . . that issues of moral responsibility and community well-being are always present in therapy and that carefully balanced attention to these issues can greatly expand the contribution of psychotherapy to the alleviation of human problems." He further maintains that therapists at times should consciously influence clients to change their behavior by considering the moral issues involved. He defines morality as those guidelines an individual already possesses including commitment, justice, truthfulness, community, caring, courage and prudence; the moral agency of the person.

The following two cases are presented to demonstrate the ways in which moral considerations might be dealt with in therapy to the benefit of the individual and society. I have used two fairly comparable situations, that of heterosexual married couples with children. The principles discussed would be similar, but not identical, with single individuals and with lesbian couples.

TWO DILEMMAS

Case 1

Sarah, after 20 years of marriage to a man who verbally and emotionally abused her, had an affair with a man her husband knew. She asserts, that out of guilt and a need for truthfulness, she told her husband about the affair, fully expecting him to (hoping he would?) throw her out. To her surprise he begged her to stay, but he accelerated his abuse and added a sexual component. After five more years of tolerating the abuse, still continuing to see the other man, she felt herself being torn in two. She was filled with guilt for her behavior and pain for her position. She finally left home at the age of 50. In the physical sense she had run from her husband, but in a psychological sense she had actually run away from her family of origin and the experiences of generations.

Sarah had grown up in a family of Holocaust survivors. The grandparents who lived with her family had visible physical and emotional scars from their imprisonment in concentration camps. As was typical of many Holocaust survivors, there was a strong commitment to others who had survived. Hers was a home where there was a steady stream of camp survivors coming to live until they could set up households on their own. Many Holocaust survivors never can allow themselves to experience joy and happiness because of survivor's guilt; it's as if they are not entitled to personal fulfillment. Sarah had internalized this message. Her role in the family had been to be the "pleaser." She smiled all the time, was the good girl and did everything asked of her. Sarah was considered the light of the family and represented their hope. She married a man who was abusive and dismissive of her from the beginning, but one whom she knew her father would adore. After her marriage she lived just blocks from her mother who came to her home every Friday night and every holiday to cook dinner while Sarah was relegated to trivial tasks. When she left her marriage, her mother continued to go to her home and cook for her husband.

Sarah was wealthy and could afford just about anything she wanted. However, she rarely had made decisions on her own and had no sense of competence because she had been infantilized by both her family of origin and her husband. She moved to a city near her two adult daughters who were very supportive of her actions. Her first task was to learn that she could take care of herself. She first set clear boundaries with her husband and her mother, refusing to speak with them until she felt strong and safe. She rented an apartment in an area that felt safe to her and rented furniture that was very different from that at home, but was what she liked. By using public transportation she explored the city, learned where the museums and theaters were, found a place of worship that she attended regularly, and found volunteer work that felt good to her. She gradually removed her large rings and other expensive jewelry and acquired items that felt more comfortable to her. Showing her new rings to me she proudly declared, "They [the stones] are from the earth." A bright, witty and attractive woman, she made friends quickly and easily. She began to research and ultimately bought a car for herself that was exactly what she wanted and symbolized to her that she could be independent. As she began to experience her competence she felt strong and happy.

However, although she had accomplished her psychological tasks of gaining autonomy, had no child responsibilities, and was financially independent, she remained torn by her family commitments. Over the course of the year her husband had gone into intensive therapy and admitted the error of his ways and promised change. He made visits to her new home and demonstrated a non-abusive way of being and expressed love and adoration of her. She agreed to visit her previous home for a short time to test his new behavior and went from home to home back and forth across the country several times in the next few months. She learned for herself that there had been changes in her husband's behavior and she also learned that she did not love her husband and did not want to be with him.

Her dilemma arose because of her original commitment to the marriage and her family/cultural value of obligation to the family unit. Her mother knew of the abuse Sarah had experienced, but still insisted that a wife's duty was to stay with her husband. She constantly chastised Sarah and shamed her for leaving. In addition, because of an extensive history of suicide in her husband's family and his serious instability (bipolar disorder), she feared for his life and was unsure of her responsibility to him. Each time she went back to her former home she was depressed and physically ill and didn't start to feel better until she had made her plane reservation to return to her new city. Still she couldn't make the break.

Sarah was an artist and had an exceptional ability to visualize things. I asked her to listen to the voices of those telling her that she was not entitled to live a life of her own choosing. Immediately she saw thousands of Holocaust victims shouting at her. When I asked her to listen closely to their words, she was surprised to find that they were telling her that her parents were wrong. The voices told her to live a full life as a way to give purpose to their death. On another occasion, when she was talking about feeling that she was being a bad girl because she wanted to continue to grow, she had an image of God telling her that it was God's wish that people live and flourish, not wither and die. I saw her images as helping her develop and evolve a belief system that would allow her to include herself in the equation of caring.

Many of her friends in both cities, as well as her children, urged her to leave her husband. They were generally critical of her for continuing to return and trying to make her marriage work. They were aware of her blossoming and *joie de vivre* when she was away from him. Yet I was very supportive of her and her decision to continue to go back and forth. I knew that she would have to gather enough information to satisfy herself that she was entitled to a happy life. I understood that the decision with which she was struggling was for her a moral one and could not be made on "objective" reality. Her decision had to come from a place in her that would allow her to live in peace with herself. I knew she would only be able to leave when she found a way that would be respectful and caring of all the people involved.

The fact is that this time allowed her, her husband and her mother to learn that she and they could survive Sarah's autonomy. They all learned that although she could not continue to live the way she had, she still had deep caring and could remain connected. She stayed in the marriage longer than most thought she should; after she knew she wanted another life and knew she could take care of herself. Nevertheless, by seeking to find a path that felt moral and responsible to her, she was ultimately able to help all the people involved and felt better about herself in the long run.

Case 2

Debbie came into therapy when she was unhappy in her marriage because her husband was alexithymic. She felt lonely and was very sad about the state of their relationship. She had been acting as the primary caretaker of three very young and behaviorally difficult children while Bob, her husband, went off to work at a traditional mid-level corporate job. Their communication was limited to taking care of life functions and lacked any semblance of intimacy. Sex had been absent from the marriage for a long time. After years of indifference to one another at one moment and then explosive arguments the next, Debbie told Bob that if he did not go into therapy, she would leave the relationship. He entered individual therapy and after he had been in therapy for about one year they began to see a couples counselor.

Although Bob made many significant changes in his behavior, Debbie never felt close to him and frequently minimized his accomplishments. As the child of alcoholic parents, she had a great deal of anger at her family of origin and often projected her anger for them onto her husband. When this happened he felt attacked and abandoned and he would often sabotage progress they had made.

Debbie came regularly to therapy and identified her distaste for the feeling of dependence she experienced in her marriage. To counter these feelings she began to develop her own business and make friends outside the marriage. Along with individual and couples therapy, she agreed to go to an intensive weekend marriage seminar recommended by the couples therapist and me. They both came away from the weekend feeling they had learned a lot, but upon returning home failed to apply the information.

Debbie was not willing to deal with her own anger with her family of origin; she blamed Bob for all her unhappiness and loneliness. Although she could acknowledge that he was working hard to make changes in his behavior and their relationship, she eventually decided that there was nothing he could do that would satisfy her. She came to the conclusion that she was no longer in love with him and never could be again. She also decided that she could not leave the marriage.

Although Debbie and Bob were not wealthy, they could have managed financially to separate or divorce. Debbie's reason for not leaving was not practical or objective, but rather based on her moral belief system. She knew that Bob loved the children and had significantly changed his behavior with them and had learned to interact with them in a healthy manner. The children loved him and enjoyed doing things with him. Debbie felt that her level of sadness and discomfort in the marriage did not warrant subjecting her children, Bob, and their respective families to the depth and breadth of pain that they would experience if she left the marriage. Although she knew her life would not be able to blossom the way she wanted, she felt it was not morally acceptable to leave.

I supported Debbie in her decision not to leave the marriage because it was clear to me that the price for leaving would have been too high for her to pay from a moral and ultimately a psychological perspective. Bob was not abusive and her life was pleasant and bearable, if not loving and growthful. She was quite clear about her lack of feelings towards Bob and she knew she would be much happier if she were on her own. Nonetheless, she would not be able to be at peace with a decision to leave because it would be incongruent with her belief system. She decided that she would not resent Bob for her decision to stay. She knew that if the marriage became significantly intolerable she could reexamine her decision. She also knew that when the children got older she would have more flexibility to expand her life either within the context of the marriage or by leaving.

DISCUSSION

The similarities in these two cases are more striking than the differences. Both women were dissatisfied in their marriages. Both persevered for a long time. Both came to the conclusion that they no longer loved the man to whom they were married. Both were strong and creative women. Both struggled with the separation because of their concern for others and because of the moral issues involved in ending a marriage. In both cases the women would have been much happier, sooner, if they had chosen to leave when they knew the marriage was not working out for them. Each found it imperative to consider the impact of their own actions on those with whom they were in relationship, i.e., children and parents as well as spouse.

These two examples demonstrate that being moral does not necessarily mean staying with, or leaving, a person one does not love. The determination is based upon an individual's belief system and the context of her life. What sometimes may appear to be a choice at the expense of self, may in fact be improvement of self. Each woman ultimately felt better about herself because of the way in which she had handled her situation.

There are ways in which each could have been encouraged and aided to make a choice to leave her marriage much earlier in the process, thereby personally avoiding much pain and suffering. Ethically it is not for the therapist to use her power to move a person in any direction other than that which the person chooses. Therapeutically and morally it is critical to bring the client's belief system into the process of decisionmaking. This must be done by either supporting the system that the client presents or helping her identify and clarify her guiding moral code. To respect an individual's autonomy we must also respect the part of their being that has a deep consideration of others. This aids not only the client and those in the immediate situation, but all future relationships of this person. By validating and supporting the moral frame of an individual when one is struggling with a decision, the therapist is contributing to an improvement in all human relationships as well as the moral agency of the individual.

It is important that feminist therapists help people to be congruent by helping them learn to integrate their own needs into a larger picture of what is good for everyone. Feminist therapists must consider the individual, her situation and her belief systems in order best to help her establish a path that is right for her rather than work from a political analysis alone when dealing with intra- and interpersonal conflicts.

REFERENCES

Brom, D. & Witztum, E. (1995). When political reality enters therapy: Ethical considerations in the treatment of posttraumatic stress disorder. In Kleber, R. & Figley, C. (Eds.). *Beyond trauma: Cultural and societal dynamics.* NY: Plenum Press.

Doherty, W.J. (1995). *Soul searching: Why psychotherapy must promote moral responsibility.* NY: Basic Books.

Erickson, R. (1989). Psychotherapy as a moral enterprise. *Pastoral Psychology.* 38(1), 25-33.

Fallon, B., Liebowitz, M., Hollander, E. & Schnier, F. (1990). The pharmacotherapy of moral or religious scrupulosity. *Journal of Clinical Psychiatry.* 51(12), 517-521.
Frank, A. (1992). The pedagogy of suffering: Moral dimensions of psychological therapy and research. *Theory and Psychology.* 2(4), 467-485.
Gibbs, J. (1993). Moral-cognitive interventions. In A. Goldstein (Ed.), *The gang intervention handbook.* Champaign: Research Press.
Hirsh, N.D. (1976). *Ethics and Human Relationships.* NY: Carlton Press.
Kitwood, T. (1990). *Concern for others: A new psychology of conscience and morality.* London: Routledge.
Lakin, M. (1994). Morality in group and family therapies: Multiperson therapies and the 1992 ethics code. *Professional Psychology: Research & Practice.* 25(4), 344-348.
Lee, J. (1997). Morality in psychoanalysis. *International Medical Journal.* 4(1), 19-23.
Lomas, P. (1997). The moral maze of psychoanalysis. In T. Dufresne (Ed.), *Freud under analysis: History, theory, practice.* NJ: Jason Aronson.
London, P. (1986). *The modes and morals of psychotherapy.* (2nd ed.) Washington, DC: Hemisphere Publishing.
Madanes, C. (1997). Shame: How to bring a sense of right and wrong into the family. In J. Zeig. (Ed.), *The evolution of psychotherapy: The third conference.* NY: Brunner/Mazel.
Mullan, H. (1991). Inherent moral practice in group psychotherapy. *International Journal of Group Psychotherapy.* 41(2), 185-197.
Nicholas, M. (1993). How to deal with moral issues in group therapy without being judgmental. *International Journal of Group Psychotherapy.* 43(2), 205-221.
Nicholas, M. (1994). *The mystery of goodness and the positive moral consequences of psychotherapy.* NY: Norton.
Prilleltensky, I. (1996). Human, moral and political values for an emancipatory psychology. *Humanistic Psychologist.* 24(3), 307-324.

Split Loyalties: The Conflicting Demands of Individual Treatment Goals and Parental Responsibility

Sally A. Keller

SUMMARY. A growing awareness of the high incidence of child abuse over the past two decades has resulted in a proliferation of preventive service agencies and a societal mandate for heightened scrutiny by mental health professionals of parenting practices. Therapists who work with families at risk increasingly walk a fine line between the individual needs of the parent and the obligation to safeguard the welfare of the child. This article presents case material in which parental responsibility and parental fitness became a central theme of treatment as a result of a child custody dispute. The article explores the intersection of personal values and morality, with legal, ethical and therapeutic considerations that arise in the context of parental responsibility. The author argues that, consistent with feminist therapy, there can and should be a place for morality in resolving therapeutic issues concerning parental responsibility. However, the author questions the extent to which the feminist commitment to empowerment of the individual can co-exist with the therapist's evaluative role concerning parental responsibility and parental fitness. *[Article copies*

Sally A. Keller, Gordon Derner Institute of Advanced Psychological Studies, Adelphi University, a doctoral student in clinical psychology, is also an attorney whose practice has included both criminal prosecution and civil litigation.

The author wishes to thank Michelle Collins, PhD, for her helpful and empathic supervision on this case.

Address correspondence to: Sally A. Keller, 43 North Drive, Great Neck, NY 11021.

[Haworth co-indexing entry note]: "Split Loyalties: The Conflicting Demands of Individual Treatment Goals and Parental Responsibility." Keller, Sally A. Co-published simultaneously in *Women & Therapy* (The Haworth Press, Inc.) Vol. 22, No. 2, 1999, pp. 117-131; and: *Beyond the Rule Book: Moral Issues and Dilemmas in the Practice of Psychotherapy* (eds: Ellyn Kaschak, and Marcia Hill) The Haworth Press, Inc., 1999, pp. 117-131. Single or multiple copies of this article are available for a fee from The Haworth Document Delivery Service [1-800-342-9678, 9:00 a.m. - 5:00 p.m. (EST). E-mail address: getinfo@haworthpress inc.com].

© 1999 by The Haworth Press, Inc. All rights reserved.

available for a fee from The Haworth Document Delivery Service: 1-800-342-9678. E-mail address: getinfo@haworthpressinc.com]

KEYWORDS. Parental responsibility, morality, empowerment

Growing awareness of the high incidence of child maltreatment has contributed to a proliferation of preventive service agencies. As regulatory reform struggles to effect a shift from crisis intervention to planned intervention, the issue of caregiving dysfunction has migrated from the courtroom to the mental health clinic. Hospitals and clinics commonly receive government funding to provide services to families at risk. While prevention is an articulated goal of family treatment, family services operate within the framework of clearly defined and increasingly stringent child welfare laws. The goals of family preservation and child protection operate concurrently in a sometimes collaborative, often antagonistic, relationship.

Despite universal agreement that the welfare of the child is of paramount importance, society's heightened scrutiny of the family has profound implications for mental health professionals. Therapists who work with families at risk struggle to maintain a balance between treatment that preserves family integrity and interventions that minimize the risk of harm to the child. Where the client is the child, involvement of protective services or the courts may further jeopardize the child's safety, while forcing at least a symbolic choice between therapist and family. Where the client is the parent, the duty to report maltreatment may place the therapist in an authoritarian and punitive role. In either case, the therapist faces split loyalties and a potential rupture of the therapeutic alliance.

Child custody is a related issue that has similarly far-reaching implications for the therapeutic setting. For families at risk, custody issues may involve foster care or guardianship placements with next of kin. Questions of whether to reunite family members arise frequently in a family treatment setting. Thus a therapist, despite every effort to avoid the role of expert witness, may nevertheless become embroiled in a courtroom custody battle. Whether providing expert opinion testimony or serving as a fact witness, the therapist in the courtroom ordinarily lacks the ability to safeguard client confidentiality. Therefore the obligation to testify in a court of law, like the mandate to report child maltreatment, may generate feelings of betrayal and inequities between therapist and client that threaten to disrupt the therapeutic relationship.

In work with adult clients, child custody and child maltreatment are perhaps the most salient examples of issues that fall under the rubric of parental responsibility. Given the societal mandate that the welfare of the child comes first, the possibility exists for every parent who is in treatment that individual needs may at some point fall prey to a higher order demand of parental responsibility. For the therapist, the conflicting demands of client needs and parental responsibility mean facing difficult, even wrenching treatment decisions in the face of ambivalent and potentially conflicting guidelines. These guidelines take several forms: (1) laws and regulations, such as the duty to report child abuse or to respond to a subpoena, for which the failure to comply may carry clear legal sanctions; (2) rules of ethics, that govern professional standards; and (3) therapeutic concerns, such as the transferential and countertransferential impact of prioritizing among family versus individual needs.

More generally, ethical decision-making involves some assessment of what is right and wrong. From a feminist perspective, right and wrong cannot be assessed solely by reference to an existing code or set of rules. Rather, ethical decision-making takes into account the values, beliefs and socio-cultural context of the people involved in the problem situation (Hill, Glaser, and Harden, 1995). Thus, according to feminist therapy, values and morality have a role in the practice of therapy.

This paper will explore the role of morality in the context of a therapy case in which parental responsibility became a central theme of treatment. The paper will argue that the therapist should and inevitably does draw on internal values to reconcile legal and ethical standards concerning parental responsibility. For the therapist, the greater struggle may not be whether or what place to accord morality, but to remain conscious of morality's sway, and to refrain from dressing personal values in the garb of an ethical or legal imperative.

The discussion will focus on Ms. T., a 33-year-old Jamaican woman of color, who began to work with me in her third year of treatment at a family services clinic at a major New York City hospital. Ms. T. initially was referred to the clinic by Child Protective Services as a condition of retaining custody of her children. At the time of her referral, she carried diagnoses of post-traumatic stress disorder and major depression.

Ms. T. is the mother of five girls, ages 2 to 7. The youngest girls are twins, both developmentally delayed. Ms. T. also has two teenage daughters being raised by her mother in Jamaica. Up until 5 years ago, Ms. T. was in a severely abusive relationship with the father of her five younger daughters. While in this relationship, she became both physically and emotionally unable to care for her children, who were temporarily taken from the home. Ms. T. was reunited with the three older girls when she moved to a shelter for battered women. She regained custody of one of her twins after she left the shelter and obtained housing. Her fifth daughter, who is more severely disabled, remained in the temporary care of the paternal grandmother.

Ms. T. related little information regarding her family history. She is the only daughter among six children born to her mother and father in Jamaica. Her father, who was 20 years older than her mother, was bedridden for several years. He died in Jamaica approximately 9 months after Ms. T. began treatment with me. Ms. T. had a brother living in New York, who had been in jail on drug charges for several years. She also had an aunt and a cousin who lived nearby, but described having been kicked out of their house when she was pregnant with her seven-year-old daughter, and being too angry to initiate contact with them. Ms. T. described her relationship with her children's paternal grandmother as acrimonious. She frequently complained that the grandmother, who was the caretaker of her youngest daughter, was turning her daughter against her.

I was Ms. T.'s third therapist in a string of one-year externs at the clinic. Ms. T. did not show up for her first two scheduled appointments, and when we finally met she wore an expression of cold fury on her face. At the time our work began, Ms. T. was interested only in what I could do for her. She was unemployed, could not afford child care, and was struggling to feed and clothe her children. She had aspirations to go to school and to get a job, but felt trapped at home. Those whom she enlisted for child care proved to be untrustworthy or unavailable. Discussions focused on Ms. T.'s concrete needs, which were many and real. What she wanted first and foremost was a home attendant who would watch her children during the day. She had a positive experience with a home attendant who had been placed with her family when she first left the shelter. This home attendant was one of the few people ever characterized by Ms. T. as caring and trustworthy.

The focus on Ms. T.'s concrete needs reflected both her environmental deprivation and the poverty of her internal experience. On a conscious level, Ms. T. saw herself as embattled against a world that was both withholding and punitive. She struggled to get her needs met, but was continually disappointed by others. She vigilantly guarded against danger, but feared that she could not protect herself from harm. Internally, Ms. T. felt hopeless, ugly and worthless. She was filled with rage at her own inefficacy, and projected her murderous feelings onto others, thus intensifying and distorting her anticipation of maltreatment. Interpersonally, Ms. T. exhibited a hypervigilance and distrust of others that reflected both her history of oppression and a splitting of her intrapsychic world. People either were all-giving, such as her previous home attendant, or totally untrustworthy, such as her jealous and conspiratorial neighbors. In treatment, I came to understand Ms. T.'s focus on her deprivation both as a request that I meet her needs, and an attempt to ascertain what I might be for her–either nurturing caregiver or purveyor of harm.

The goals of treatment in this case were manifold. From a preventive services perspective, the central goal of therapy was to address the impulsive anger and depression that impaired Ms. T.'s parenting skills. More generally, however, Ms. T. worked to develop a sense of agency and self-worth. An integral part of this work was to help Ms. T. to integrate the various split-off aspects of herself and others, so that her world could become less polarized, allowing her to develop the capacity to form relationships based on mutuality and acceptance. These various treatment goals were not in and of themselves contradictory. However, to the extent that treatment addressed itself to the integrity of the family, it also contained an implicitly evaluative component that fed Ms. T.'s hypervigilance and distrust.

Early in our work together, I attempted to allay Ms. T.'s distrust by tacitly affirming her parental role. Since child care was unavailable to Ms. T., she regularly brought her children with her to the clinic. At the start of each session, I would engage the children in conversation or activities while discussing their likes and dislikes with Ms. T. At the same time, I would concur with Ms. T.'s observations concerning the unending work of raising children. From the outset, it appeared that while Ms. T. wanted me to acknowledge her family, she was reluctant to share her therapy time with them.

Gradually, Ms. T.'s parenting became an increasing focus of the treatment. During the therapy session, the two youngest girls wandered in and out of the room unsupervised. Ms. T.'s interactions with her children were often angry and inappropriate. She would snap at them to leave each other alone or order them to stop bothering her. Though her tone of voice was threatening, she did little to effect compliance. Usually her children continued doing what they were doing, and she either ignored them or became more irritated. On one occasion, for example, her two-year-old reached into my pocketbook and began to pull things out. Ms. T. told her to stop, but the activity continued while Ms. T. sat silently in her chair. I asked her child for the bag, took it gently from her hand, and moved it out of reach. I told her that she could play with any toys she wished. Ms. T. said that her daughter didn't understand what I had said. I asked if Ms. T. felt I'd been scolding her daughter, and she said yes, that I'd sounded angry. I asked whether Ms. T. felt I'd been criticizing her parenting, and she nodded yes. We discussed how important it is that others think she is a good mother.

Later in that same session, Ms. T. revealed that her boyfriend had told her not to hit her kids. I asked about the hitting, and she said that she slaps them on the hand, otherwise they don't listen. When I questioned whether there might be other ways to get their attention, she commented that I obviously didn't have children, otherwise I would know that "you have to hit them sometimes" (in fact, at the beginning of treatment, Ms. T. had learned that I had two children). Ms. T. then voiced concern about a woman who had been babysitting her 5-year-old daughter. She said that the woman drove her daughter around " 'til all hours," and she suspected that the woman was smoking crack. I said that I thought that this was cause for extreme concern, and we discussed the dangers of entrusting her daughter to this woman's care. Finally, at the end of the session, her two-year-old opened the door and wandered into the hallway. She called her back, but did not get up from her chair. Someone in the hallway asked if she wanted the child in the room. Ms. T. said yes, but again did not rise from her seat. I told her that if she wanted her daughter back in the room, she would have to go get her. The session conveyed to me conflicting messages. Ms. T.

seemed at once to be warning me not to impinge on her parental authority, while at the same time asking for my help in this regard.

It was against this backdrop that Ms. T., about three months into treatment, told me that she would be going to court for a review of the custody arrangement for her fifth daughter, who was then in the care of the paternal grandmother. She accused the grandmother of keeping her child in order to receive the supplemental security income to which her daughter's disability entitled her. She also stressed that she was the mother, and that it was "right" for her daughter to live with her. Ms. T. asked whether I would write a letter on her behalf, saying that she was in treatment at the clinic. I provided her with a letter stating that she had come regularly to the clinic for treatment for the past three years. Ms. T. arrived for the next session with only ten minutes' time remaining. She was very angry that the letter did not contain a recommendation that her daughter be returned to her. She said that she did not know if she would come back the following week. I told her that I could see how angry and betrayed she was feeling, and that I hoped she would come back because our work together was important to me.

Ms. T. did continue in treatment, and in the spring I received a subpoena seeking documents relevant to Ms. T.'s treatment. The subpoena was issued at the behest of a psychologist appointed by the court to evaluate the parental fitness of Ms. T. and the paternal grandmother. After discussing the subpoena with Ms. T., Ms. T.'s attorney, and the court-appointed psychologist, it was agreed that I would produce copies of quarterly treatment summaries for the previous year. The summaries contained relatively little information, but discussed Ms. T.'s progress in managing her anger and depression. This time, Ms. T. was angry that I had revealed what she considered to be irrelevant and confidential information. Although we had devoted considerable time to discussing the limits of confidentiality in connection with the custody case, Ms. T. continued to believe that I could advocate on her behalf without disclosing the substance of our work together.

Finally, Ms. T. asked whether I would testify on her behalf at an upcoming custody hearing. I explained to Ms. T. that I could not simply limit my testimony to the desired recommendation that she be awarded custody. Unable to convince her that my testimony might jeopardize our working alliance, I was forced to make a decision about whether I was willing to testify on her behalf. I searched hard for a reason that would allow me to support her, questioning my prejudices and biases, while reviewing what I knew of Ms. T.'s parenting skills and current level of functioning. With much trepidation, I finally told her that I could not recommend that she be awarded custody, because I did not think that she was ready to handle the care of another child, especially one with a disability.

The expert witness in the custody case interviewed Ms. T. at length. He found her to be palpably angry, depressed, and questioned her parental fitness. Based on his assessment of both Ms. T. and the paternal grandmother, he recommended that the grandmother continue as custodian, and the judge followed his recommendation.

LEGAL AND ETHICAL GUIDELINES

Legal and ethical guidelines provided a framework for my decision not to testify. Legally, my testimony was not compelled, since it was Ms. T., rather than the opposing counsel, who sought to call me as a witness. Having made clear that my recommendation would be unfavorable to Ms. T., it was a certainty that Ms. T.'s attorney would not seek to call me as a witness.

A more central concern was that of confidentiality. According to generally applicable rules of evidence, the client ordinarily holds a "privilege" that protects against the disclosure of confidential information about the therapy treatment. However, the client may be deemed to have waived the privilege by putting his or her mental state at issue in a court of law. In this case, if Ms. T. called me to testify on her behalf, she would be deemed to have waived her privilege with respect to the confidentiality of our work together. On cross-examination, the opposing counsel would be entitled to question me about my recommendation concerning Ms. T.'s parental fitness. Since my knowledge of Ms. T. and of our work together would have formed the basis for my opinion regarding her fitness, this information would be a proper subject of inquiry. Therefore, if Ms. T. called me as a witness, I would not be able to protect the confidentiality of information gathered in the privacy of the therapeutic relationship.

Ethically, my decision was informed by the standards set forth in the Ethical Principles and Code of Conduct of the American Psychological Association (APA), hereinafter called the Ethics Code (1992). Most generally, the Ethics Code requires psychologists to minimize the risk of harm to the client (standard 1.14, 1992). One such risk stems from dual and conflicting obligations such as that incurred by a therapist who also becomes a witness. Where dual roles may arise, the therapist is directed to clarify for the client the limits of confidentiality and the probable uses of information obtained by the court or other third parties (Ethics Code, standard 1.21(a),(b), 1992).

In the APA Commentary on the Ethics Code (1994), standard 1.21(b) is followed by a discussion of a situation in which a psychologist acts as an expert witness in a custody dispute to which his or her client is a party. The discussion focuses on the inherent conflict between the role of therapist, in which the client's welfare and confidentiality are paramount, and that of expert witness, where findings must be "based on the data, in light of the welfare of the children, even though these findings might not be in the therapy client's best interests" (APA Commentary on the Ethics Code, 1994, p. 57). With respect to Ms. T., it was my conclusion that to support her bid for custody in a court of law would compel me to disregard the welfare of her child. Since I could not reconcile her interests with those of her child, I concluded that I could not ethically take on the dual role of therapist and witness.

I was tempted to boost the ethical grounds for my decision by arguing that Ms. W. might in fact be harmed by a custody decision in her favor. It was difficult to conceive how Ms. T. could add the care of a disabled child to her already overwhelming responsibilities without risking a further decline into depression. However, Ms. T. had made clear that her identity as a mother, regardless of her parenting skills, was one of the few defining features of her fragile sense of self. The fact that custody would bring her monthly SSI payments also could not be discounted, although it might seem a crude measure of well-being. Ultimately, legal and ethical guidelines provided a sufficient but not a necessary basis for my decision not to testify on behalf of Ms. T. The fact that I could argue both sides of the coin fueled my concern that the decision, though legally and ethically correct, might not be the "right" one.

THERAPEUTIC CONSIDERATIONS

Therapeutic considerations revolved around my safeguarding the privacy of the therapeutic relationship, on the one hand, and preserving the working alliance, on the other hand. I was deeply concerned that the waiver of privilege would result in the exposure of therapeutic content that would leave Ms. T. feeling humiliated and betrayed. I also believed that an effective cross-examination would in any event reveal my doubts about her parental fitness. Discussing my concerns in the privacy of the therapy session seemed to pose a far lesser risk of harm or exploitation than did the alternative of acceding to my client's request to testify.

As expected, however, the decision not to testify on my client's behalf had a resounding impact on the course of therapy. Initially, Ms. T. was irate and missed several sessions in a row. Gradually, she returned to therapy, but remained reserved, angry and distrustful. During this time I was required to schedule a home visit with Ms. T. Although I confirmed the visit 24 hours in advance, Ms. T. did not answer the door when I arrived at her apartment. Both my supervisor and I heard her voice coming from within. At the next session, Ms. T. informed me that she had missed the visit because she had fallen asleep. I confronted her with the fact that I had heard her voice, and she said that she felt that I was acting "like the police." We talked about Ms. T.'s experience of me as punitive and suspicious. In fact, I had been angry and confrontational about her refusal to answer the door. Ms. T.'s provocative behavior and my reaction gave shape to her internal experience, in which she was both aggressor and aggressed upon.

This episode also clarified my sense that Ms. T. had not really heard my repeated explanations regarding the limits of confidentiality in a custody proceeding. Her experience of me as "the police" left her assured that my explanation was simply another form of betrayal. Had I really wanted to protect her, I would simply have refused to disclose any information that might have caused the court to look upon her unfavorably.

For Ms. T., the wish for me to protect her may have reflected my transferential role as the good parent that she never had; the parent who would love her and approve of her even if she was bad or inadequate. By contrast, in the aftermath of my home visit, I became the harsh and critical parent who seems to have dominated her past experience. Transferentially, Ms. T. may have set me up to be the cold, judgmental parent while hoping against hope that I might turn around and take her side in spite of everything.

As the treatment progressed, I came to understand that the "police" symbolized not just the legal system, but also a ruthless assault on Ms. T.'s identity as a parent. Ms. T.'s refusal to answer the door for a home visit was both a concrete manifestation of her persecutory fears, and an aggressive assertion of her territorial rights as parent. As I began to understand the role of aggression in Ms. T.'s response to my decision not to testify, I also became more conscious of my own countertransferential feelings of guilt and shame: guilt because, by passing judgment on the adequacy of Ms. T.'s parental fitness, I could thereby implicitly affirm the superiority of my own parenting abilities; shame because I feared that I might be punishing Ms. T. for that kernel of myself that has at times wanted to shake my own small children to their senses.

The therapeutic implications of my decision were further complicated by the issue of race. I am White and Ms. T. is a woman of color. In retrospect, I believe that racism fueled the fire of anger and guilt in the therapy relationship. I unfortunately never explicitly addressed the issue of race with Ms. T. I can only assume that this unacknowledged chasm in our experiences of life added a dimension to Ms. T.'s sense of betrayal that was for me unknowable. I am certain that my own feelings of guilt were intensified by my failure to take on this aspect of nonmutuality between myself and Ms. T.

Ultimately, out of the immediacy of the transferential and countertransferential material emerged the possibility for growth. Growth came first and foremost in the survival of the therapeutic relationship. Ms. T. had shown me that her parental identity was a core component of her self-construct. This achingly vulnerable part of herself also was a potential source of strength. Together, we began to focus on the ways in which she demonstrated parental competence. We discussed how much effort went into ensuring that her children were clean and well-dressed before going to school; how she took her children everywhere because she liked for others to see her as a parent; and how she regularly brought her 7-year-old for therapy at the clinic. By knitting together some of the fabric of her self that had been torn asunder, Ms. T. gradually was able to begin to talk about how her anger interfered with and jeopardized her parental fitness. In parallel process, we addressed the possibility that hate and caring, destruction and reparation might co-exist in one and the same parent; in one and the same working alliance.

MORALITY

The unfolding of the therapeutic relationship also spawned an awareness in me of the primacy that I afforded my own internal values in my decision-making process. My personal values are informed by my identity as a White, middle class professional who also is the parent of young children. Inevitably, despite all conscious efforts to the contrary, my identity is in many ways inseparable from my morality. Thus I believe that the parent of a young child bears the ultimate responsibility for the child's well-being, and that a parent's affection, consistency, responsiveness and praise all are critical components in the development of a child's sense of security and self-esteem.

The impression I and others formed at the clinic was that anger and unpredictability pervaded Ms. T.'s parental interactions. Although nothing reportable ever was substantiated, the therapeutic narrative confirmed personal observations concerning the ways in which depression and impulsive anger jeopardized the welfare of Ms. T.'s children. Clearly, my decision was the product of a normative judgment concerning Ms. T.'s capabilities as a mother. But that judgment emerged out of its own racial, cultural, socioeconomic and personal biases. Undoubtedly, Ms. T.'s belief that children need to be hit and her stern parenting style reflects the norm in many cultures other than white, middle class America. Similarly, the task of mothering five children, while seemingly overwhelming, may be commonplace and even expected among Jamaican women of color. Curiously, I did not specifically address the issue of cultural differences with Ms. T. Perhaps I felt that she might hear such an inquiry as condoning parenting practices that I felt were harmful to her children. Perhaps I was unwilling to adjust my expectations according to cultural norms with which I was uncomfortable. Thus although I still stand by my decision not to support Ms. T.'s custody bid, it has become increasingly evident to me that my doubts concerning Ms. T.'s parental fitness were heavily influenced by my own morality.

CONSIDERATIONS FOR FEMINIST THERAPY

Perhaps a more critical question is whether my decision regarding Ms. T.'s parental fitness violated some higher order morality that recognizes individual autonomy and the right not to be subjected to another person's values. Feminist therapy is a field that has as its core concern the ethics of practice. Ethics, as construed by feminist therapists, encompass a broad political and social agenda, and are based on a commitment to change the oppression inherent in patriarchal, western societies (e.g., Larsen and Rave, 1995). A central focus of feminist ethics is empowerment. It is the responsibility of feminist therapists to address the effects of oppression in the lives of those with whom they work. In order to accomplish this goal, feminist therapists work toward equalizing the "power differential in the therapist/client relationship" (Feminist Therapy Institute, 1987, preamble).

In the case of Ms. T., disempowerment pervaded her daily existence, interpersonal relationships, and intrapsychic experience. Socioeconomic status, past abusive relationships and pathology all coincided to perpetuate Ms. T.'s sense of oppression. Power differentials in the therapeutic relationship echoed those in her daily life. Section IIA of the Feminist Code of Ethics directs that a feminist therapist

> acknowledges the inherent power differentials between client and therapist and models effective use of personal power. In using the power differential to the benefit of the client, she does not take control of power which rightfully belongs to her client.

The question presented in the context of feminist therapy is whether my decision not to support my client's bid for custody was in effect a revictimization. Clearly, Ms. T. experienced it as such when she likened me to the police. Did the decision whether to waive confidentiality rightfully belong to Ms. T.? Having repeatedly explained the risks posed by my testimony to the sanctity of the therapeutic relationship, did I then have an ethical obligation to back my client up in the face of a seemingly monolithic judicial system?

I argue that, in this case, the tenets of feminist ethics ran headlong into the thicket of parental responsibility. Conoley and Larsen (1995) pose a number of ethical dilemmas concerning conflicts in child care. One respondent in the Conoley and Larsen paper notes the omission in the Feminist Code of Ethics of a specific guideline regarding the reporting of child abuse. A second respondent addresses the "fine line the therapist must walk, not to take control of power that rightfully belongs to the client and to model effective and respectful use of power as necessary for the child's safety" (Conoley and Larsen, 1995, p. 215).

I cannot say whether my decision was "necessary" for the safety of Ms. T.'s child. However, my own sense of morality compelled my decision that I could not risk this child's welfare, even for the sake of empowering my client. On the other hand, I was aware that my client perceived me to be wresting power that belonged to her. By directly addressing Ms. T. with my doubts about her parenting, I attempted at least to model a respectful use of power-one that was honest and invited her to voice her feelings of rage and victimization.

CONCLUSION

The challenges posed by the case of Ms T. demonstrate some of the ways in which morality insinuates itself into therapeutic decisions. It is my position that the therapist bears responsibility-morally, as well as legally and ethically-to determine whether the safety of a child can be preserved within the family setting. At the same time, it may often be impossible to fulfill this responsibility without wresting power from the client in a way that contravenes the feminist ethic of mutuality and equality.

On the other hand, I believe that Ms. T. ultimately was "empowered" through her treatment in at least two respects. First, the therapy session became a safe place in which Ms. T. could vent her rage over feelings of oppression. My decision not to testify was in fact the catalyst for addressing the inherent power differentials in our relationship. Second, the custody dispute resulted in a move toward a more realistic assessment by Ms. T. of her parental strengths and weaknesses, thus generating a sense of efficacy regarding areas of parental competence, and increasing the likelihood that the court will find her fit to regain custody of her daughter at some time in the future. Does this constitute empowerment in terms of feminist ethics? If not, perhaps the next step for feminist therapy is to address the obstacles to empowerment posed by the issue of parental responsibility. One way to do this might be to ensure that this issue, like that of ethnic and cultural differences, is discussed openly in the course of treatment. It might be that empowerment in this arena can emerge from honest disagreement between therapist and client over how best to reconcile the individual needs of the client with the welfare of the child.

REFERENCES

American Psychological Association. (1992). *Ethical principles and code of conduct.* Washington, DC: Author.

American Psychological Association. (1994). *Ethics for psychologists: A commentary on the APA Ethics Code.* Canter, M.B., Bennett, B.E., Jones, S.E. & Nagy, T.F. (Eds.) Washington, DC: Author.

Conoley, J.C., & Larson, P. (1995). Conflicts in care: Early years of the lifespan. In E.J. Rave & C.C. Larsen (Eds.), *Ethical decision-making in therapy* (pp. 202-222). New York: The Guilford Press.

Feminist Therapy Institute, 1987. *Feminist therapy code of ethics.* Denver: Author.

Hill, M., Glaser, K., & Harden, J. (1995). A feminist model for ethical decision making. In E.J. Rave & C.C. Larsen (Eds.), *Ethical decision-making in therapy* (pp. 18-37). New York: The Guilford Press.

Larsen, C.C. & Rave, E.J. (1995). Context of feminist therapy ethics. In E.J. Rave & C.C. Larsen (Eds.), *Ethical decision-making in therapy* (pp. 1-17). New York: The Guilford Press.

The Moral Imperative: Self-Care for Women Psychotherapists

Lynne Carroll
Paula J. Gilroy
Jennifer Murra

SUMMARY. Given recent evidence concerning the prevalence of impairment in practitioners and its deleterious effects upon clients, therapist self-care must be viewed as a moral imperative. Despite the perception that self-care is especially problematic for women psychotherapists, research indicates that we are less ambivalent about practicing self-care and engaging in personal therapy than men practitioners (Mahoney, 1997). We propose a classification system based upon the dimensions of awareness of impairment and commitment to self-care and offer practical suggestions in order to create a climate more amenable for women therapists to engage in self-care activities. *[Article copies available for a fee from The Haworth Document Delivery Service: 1-800-342-9678. E-mail address: getinfo@haworthpressinc.com]*

KEYWORDS. Self-care, women psychotherapists, ethics, feminist therapy

---

Lynne Carroll, PhD, is Assistant Professor in the Counselor Education Program at the University of North Florida. Paula J. Gilroy, EdD, is a psychologist at the University of Northern Iowa Counseling Center. Jennifer Murra, MA, NCC, is a mental health counselor at the University of Northern Iowa Counseling Center.

Address correspondence to: Lynne Carroll, Counselor Education Program, University of North Florida, 4567 St. Johns Bluff Road, South, Jacksonville, FL 32224-2676. Electronic mail may be sent via Internet to LCARROLL@UNF.EDU.

[Haworth co-indexing entry note]: "The Moral Imperative: Self-Care for Women Psychotherapists." Carroll, Lynne, Paula J. Gilroy, and Jennifer Murra. Co-published simultaneously in *Women & Therapy* (The Haworth Press, Inc.) Vol. 22, No. 2, 1999, pp. 133-143; and: *Beyond the Rule Book: Moral Issues and Dilemmas in the Practice of Psychotherapy* (eds: Ellyn Kaschak, and Marcia Hill) The Haworth Press, Inc., 1999, pp. 133-143. Single or multiple copies of this article are available for a fee from The Haworth Document Delivery Service [1-800-342-9678, 9:00 a.m. - 5:00 p.m. (EST). E-mail address: getinfo@haworthpressinc.com].

© 1999 by The Haworth Press, Inc. All rights reserved.

In recent years there has been a burgeoning interest in distress and impairment in mental health practitioners (e.g., Guy, Poelstra, & Stark, 1989; Sherman, 1996; Sherman & Thelen, 1998; etc.). This research has not only heightened our awareness of the need to shift focus beyond the recognition of distress and impairment in professionals to the advocation of self-care and well-functioning (e.g., Coster & Schwebel, 1997; Schwebel & Coster, 1998). As Porter (1995) observed, we are in the midst of a paradigm shift from an exclusive focus on the care and well-being of clients to the care and well-being of ourselves as well as our clients. The inclusion of self-care guidelines within the Feminist Therapy Institute Code of Ethics (Feminist Therapy Institute, 1990) represents a significant attempt to move beyond the view of self-care as merely a form of self-indulgence or personal luxury. Solomon (1984) argued that ethical principles can be distinguished from moral ones, in that the latter represent the basic, universal, and inviolable rules of society. Among those key moral duties identified by philosopher Ross (1930) were beneficence and nonmaleficence. In light of the compelling evidence concerning the prevalence of impairment in practitioners and its deleterious effects upon clients, therapist self-care must be viewed not only as an ethical principle, but a moral imperative. In this article we explore the following issues: (1) the symptoms and incidence of distress and impairment in mental health practitioners; (2) the question of whether it is especially problematic for women therapists to engage in self-care activities; (3) a typology of clinicians which addresses the dimensions of self-awareness of distress, impairment, and engagement in self-care activities; and (4) a mandate for self-care which includes specific recommendations for the individual practitioner as well as the profession.

DISTRESS AND IMPAIRMENT AMONG PRACTITIONERS

Research has identified the numerous signs and symptoms of distress in mental health practitioners: irritability, depression, boredom, withdrawal, loss of energy, feelings of failure, somatic complaints, lowered self-esteem, and decreased exercise (Coster & Schwebel, 1997; Mahoney, 1997; Prochaska & Norcross, 1983). Depression is one prevalent form of distress found among mental health practitioners. In their survey of psychologists, Pope and Tabachnick (1994) found that 61% of their sample had experienced at least one episode of clinical depression. In our recent survey of women mental health practitioners, 76% reported personal experiences with some form of depression (Gilroy, Carroll, & Murra, 1998). Distress in practitioners is reported to be quite high, with as many as 60% of survey respondents admitting to levels of distress which caused them to work beyond their levels of effectiveness (Pope, Tabachnick, & Keith-Spiegel, 1987). It is important to note that although distressed practitioners admit to their distress, this does not necessarily mean that they practice self-care or that their distress impairs their work with clients.

Sherman and Thelen (1998) defined impairment as "the interference in the ability to practice therapy, which may be sparked by a variety of factors and results in a decline in therapeutic effectiveness" (p. 79). Sherman (1996) cited three categories of impairment which include substance abuse, sexual misconduct, and emotional problems/mental health issues. Possible indicators of impairment include poor clinical judgment, greater risk of ethical breaches such as boundary violations, power abuses, and inappropriate emotional involvement with clients (Faunce, 1990; Porter, 1995). Impaired practitioners differ from distressed practitioners in that they do not typically recognize their impairment (Nathan, 1986). For example, Guy et al. (1989) indicated that those respondents who reported substance abuse denied any impact of their substance use/abuse on their clinical work. In their study of licensed psychologists, Wood, Klein, Cross, Lammers and Elliott (1985) found that "approximately 40% are aware of colleagues whose work is affected by the use of drugs or sexual overtures, and over 60% state the same for depression or burnout" (p. 846).

SELF-CARE DEFINED

Self-care is defined as the integration of the following elements: physical, cognitive, emotional, play, and spiritual (Faunce, 1990; Moursund, 1993; Porter, 1995). Based upon our review of the literature, such self-care activities may be clustered into four categories which include: intrapersonal work, interpersonal support, professional development and support, and physical/recreational activities. Porter (1995) delineated the following three primary functions served by self-care: (a) protection of the therapist by reducing occupational hazards such as burnout; (b) enhancement of therapy by modeling healthy behavior; and (c) protection of the client by reducing risks of ethical violations.

Empirical attempts have been made to delineate self-care activities which are most frequently utilized by mental health practitioners and those which are perceived as most effective. The first category, intrapersonal work, referred to increasing self-awareness through personal therapy, spirituality or consciousness-raising groups, adhering to personal values, and maintaining a balanced lifestyle and a sense of humor (Kramen-Kahn & Hansen, 1998; Porter, 1995; Schwebel & Coster, 1998). The second category, interpersonal support, involved maintaining healthy spouse/significant other and family relationships, friendships, and collegial relationships (Kramen-Kahn & Hansen, 1998; Schwebel & Coster, 1998). The third category, professional development and support, included such activities as using case consultation, scheduling breaks during the day, attending continuing education seminars, monitoring caseloads in size and types of cases, and setting realistic expectations at work (Faunce, 1990; Kramen-Kahn & Hansen, 1998; Sherman & Thelen, 1998). The fourth category, physical/recreational activities, involved pursuing non-work related activities, leisure activities, regular exercise, reading, hobbies, and recreational vacations (Kramen-Kahn & Hansen, 1998; Mahoney, 1997; Sherman & Thelen, 1998).

IS SELF-CARE PROBLEMATIC FOR WOMEN PSYCHOTHERAPISTS?

Psychotherapists engage in activities which emphasize the care of and well-being of others. In effect, clients' needs are paramount, regardless of the emotional and physical consequences to therapists. Mainstream practices discourage and even stigmatize self-care. Common behavioral patterns noted among practitioners which may exemplify a lack of self-care include: (a) seeing potentially dangerous clients in deserted premises, (b) socially isolating oneself, (c) neglecting meal breaks, (d) masochistically putting the client's needs first, and (e) maintaining a constant sitting position and therefore experiencing recurrent back problems (Marigson, 1997).

Women, whether or not they are psychotherapists, often regard the practice of self-care as self-serving and therefore a failure to meet socialized expectations. The priorization of other-care over self-care is embedded in the cultural experiences of girls and women and in the training process for psychotherapists. Yet, interestingly, current research indicates that women therapists are just as likely as men therapists to engage in self-care activities such as pleasure reading, exercise, and peer supervision (Kramen-Kahn & Hansen, 1998; Mahoney, 1997; Sherman & Thelen, 1998). Research has also demonstrated that women clinicians seek personal therapy significantly more often than do men clinicians (e.g., Kramen-Kahn & Hansen, 1998; Mahoney, 1997; Norcross, Strausser-Kirtland, & Missar, 1988; Norman & Rosvall, 1994). In our survey of women mental health practitioners, 85% of respondents who had reported experiencing depressive symptoms sought personal therapy (Gilroy, Carroll, & Murra, 1998). It is plausible to suggest that this commitment to self-care, including personal therapy, may also be an artifact of the greater reported professional distress women clinicians experience as a result of their multiple caretaking roles (e.g., Sherman & Thelen, 1998) and the propensity noted in women in general to seek personal therapy (Brodsky & Hare-Mustin, 1980).

A TYPOLOGY OF PSYCHOTHERAPISTS' AWARENESS OF IMPAIRMENT AND COMMITMENT TO SELF-CARE

Based upon our research and personal observations we propose a classification system which delineates three basic types of clinicians. This system represents a means of assisting women therapists in recognizing differing forms of distress, impairment, and engagement in self-care activities both in themselves and in their colleagues. Our schema is organized around two principle axes: (a) self-awareness regarding one's level of distress and impairment and (b) personal commitment to self-care.

The first type, entitled "aware/committed," refers to clinicians who are aware of their mental health problems and act to safeguard themselves from continuing improper, unethical, and ineffectual therapy practices. Aware/committed therapists understand that self-care on the part of the therapist serves to enhance growth and self-care on the part of the client (Porter, 1995). These therapists firmly believe that to not practice self-care is to risk harming the client. They regularly practice self-care strategies including exercise, meditation, peer supervision, personal time, relaxation, proper sleep, and nutrition. These strategies are often sufficient to maintain therapists' wellness which in turn facilitates sound therapy practices. In addition, such clinicians are open to seeking personal therapy when appropriate.

The second type, entitled "aware/uncommitted," refers to clinicians who are aware of their mental health issues, but do not act to effect change. Such practitioners do not routinely incorporate self-care activities into their daily lives. Regarding self-care practices other than personal therapy, aware/uncommitted therapists disregard self-care for many reasons including: (a) lack of time and energy, (b) the perception of clients' needs as paramount to their own, and (c) a minimization of the effectiveness of self-care. With respect to personal therapy, aware/uncommitted therapists perceive therapy as evidence of personal "failure." The aware/uncommitted therapist "sees unsureness, self-doubt, and confusion as marks of inadequacy and even a kind of therapist sinfulness" (Blau, 1984; p. 9). Clinicians of this type work in the grey zone; that fine line between ethical and unethical conduct. The extent to which they practice unethically is likely related to the client's presenting issues and their relevance to the therapist's personal issues. Such therapists are vulnerable to commit boundary violations termed by Brown (1991) as "failure to protect" where therapists are either "too sloppy or fuzzy" in their own boundaries or where therapists neglect or ignore important treatment issues.

The third type, entitled "unaware/uncommitted," refers to clinicians who appear oblivious to their own mental health issues and impairment, and therefore run the highest risk of unethical conduct. Such therapists provoke the greatest level of concern because they are particularly vulnerable to commit boundary violations, which Brown (1991) termed "invasive violations," in which the client's physical or emotional boundaries are breached either through intrusion or engulfment. Therapists who deny personal problems risk exploitation of clients for their own needs, leaving clients dependent and powerless. To illustrate this, we offer a case from our own experience, which involved a therapist who was providing clinical supervision at our agency. It was obvious to both staff and student interns that this therapist/supervisor was practicing while under the influence of alcohol. Not only were the trainees affected by his unpredictable mood and his unprofessional language, but the trainee's clients were also affected by the lack of appropriate feedback. The supervisor's inappropriate behavior led to a series of confrontations which were extremely frustrating, given the supervisor's consistent denial of any unethical behavior.

There may be a subset of individuals within this type who participate in self-care activities and even outspokenly advocate that therapists seek therapy when necessary. Margison (1997) noted that therapists working with other therapists observe that even obvious indicators of distress (e.g., increase in alcohol consumption, use of drugs, etc.) were often ignored by their therapist clients. To illustrate this type, we offer an example from our own experience which involved a mental health practitioner who inappropriately disclosed her own abuse history to her client. Eventually a personal relationship developed. Whether or not sexual misconduct occurred could not be proven, though sufficient evidence was present to prompt suspicion. The therapist openly discussed her personal therapy and other forms of self-care including meditation and exercise, but she lacked the behavioral commitment necessary for effective self-care. It seemed that talking about self-care and even attending therapy sessions were more for the sake of appearance than a genuine desire to take responsibility for her own issues.

RECOMMENDATIONS FOR THE PROFESSION

The commitment to self-care and the call to action within the mental health profession must occur at both individual and systemic levels. We propose that professional organizations assume a more aggressive stance in terms of mandating self-care. The FTI Code of Ethics (Feminist Therapy Institute, 1990) is the only professional code which contains specific reference to self-care. Other professional organizations (e.g., American Psychological Association and the American Counseling Association) must follow the example of feminists in this regard. Other recommendations include the regular provision of continuing education credits for participation in self-care activities, personal therapy, and educative workshops on topics like distress, impairment, and self-care.

At the institutional level, the current focus within counselor training programs on skill building is insufficient. It is imperative for trainees to be aware of their own personal issues and be willing to engage in self-care activities including personal therapy. While most counselor educators believe that personal psychotherapy during the training process is a recommended experience (e.g., Coster & Schwebel, 1997), most stop short in terms of requiring it. In their survey of programs in professional psychology, Schwebel and Coster (1998) found that the most often cited programmatic changes desired by department chairs in order to better ensure the future well-functioning of their graduates was required therapy.

While the curriculum across the country in most counselor training programs contains a course in ethics, little attention is paid to the issues of self-care and risk factors. Porter (1995) advocated that we not only educate therapists about ethical standards and potential abuses, but the risk factors which facilitate abuses. Tools, like the typology of awareness of impairment and commitment to self-care presented here, represent useful ways of assisting trainees to explore their own behavioral patterns and to heighten their sensitivity to the need for self-care. Several authors (e.g., Kramen-Kahn & Hansen, 1998; Schwebel & Coster, 1998) advocated the inclusion of a professional self-care course which is taught as part of the formal curriculum and includes topics such as (a) stress management training, (b) barriers to obtaining support, (c) working in teams, and (d) personal issues in working with clients.

Cushway (1996) proposed a supervision model which is the first to contain a comprehensive approach to teaching self-care during psychotherapy training. The model includes the following components: (a) a philosophy adopted by supervisors which recognizes and normalizes personal stress; (b) organizational flexibility in adapting work responsibilities to the needs of the trainee; and (c) the establishment of support systems for trainees including a tutor who functions outside the training program and confidential personal awareness groups facilitated by outside professionals. The major distinction between Cushway's (1996) and other models of supervision is the inclusion of self-care practices as an integral part of the supervisory process. Although earlier models recommended self-care (e.g., Stoltenberg, 1981) for the purpose of improving trainees' therapeutic skills, we agree with Cushway's (1996) emphasis on self-care with the goal of trainees' increased ability to recognize their own distress and subsequently to practice self-care. The integration of self-care into the supervision process acknowledges the trainee as human which hopefully reduces the stigma associated with mental health professionals engaging in self-care. Research does show that those mental health practitioners who were exposed to personal therapy during their early years as professionals, were more amenable to seeking therapy later in their careers when distressed or experiencing emotional problems (Pope et al., 1994).

While research (Mahoney, 1997; Porter, 1995) clearly indicated that practitioners value personal therapy, it is also evident that strong fears and avoidance behaviors accompany the prospect of personal therapy. Clearly, some of these fears are not unfounded. In our survey of women mental health practitioners (Gilroy, Carroll, & Murra, 1998), it was interesting to note a high percentage of respondents who described feeling judged and ostracized by colleagues who learned of their depression. Walsh, Nichols, and Cormack's (1991) study of psychotherapists revealed that most were reluctant to use their colleagues for personal support at work. Foremost among their reasons was the belief that they would be stigmatized for their problems, and their perception of colleagues as untrustworthy. In general, it appears that the internalized belief that therapists must epitomize positive mental health runs deep in the psyches of many practitioners. The issue of shame in mental health practitioners is one worth exploring in greater depth (Sussman, 1995).

CONCLUSION

Given the documented high incidence of distress and impairment in mental health professionals, self-care must become a moral imperative. Research seems to suggest, however, that women therapists, especially feminist therapists, are less ambivalent about practicing self-care and engaging in personal therapy. In order for self-care to become a mandate for the profession as a whole, a number of systemic changes must take place like the inclusion of self-care guidelines in all professional codes of ethics, mandatory therapy for trainees, new models of supervision, and curriculum revisions. It is clear that the mandate for self-care has the potential to lessen the negative stigma attached to the use of personal therapy among clinicians, facilitate an increase in the numbers of therapists who routinely practice self-care, and encourage professionals to confront colleagues who do not engage in self-care. Caution is needed, however, in terms of searching for quick fixes to the problem of distress and impairment in practitioners. Brown (1994) admonished us that self-care does not merely mean dutifully following a set of prescribed activities like exercise and meditation, it means "to continually ask whether and how one is practicing this principle" (p. 213). In the words of one therapist: "Your competence as a therapist cannot exceed your competence as a human being" (Moursund, 1993; p. 217).

REFERENCES

Blau, T.H. (1984). Preface. In F.W. Kaslow (Ed.), *In psychotherapy with psychotherapists* (pp. 8-9). New York: Haworth.

Brodsky, A.M. & Hare-Mustin, R.T. (1980). (Eds)., *Women and psychotherapy: An assessment of research and practice.* New York: Guilford Press.

Brown, L.S. (1991). Ethical issues in feminist therapy. *Psychology of Women Quarterly, 15*, 323-336.

Brown, L.S. (1994). *Subversive dialogues.* New York: Basic Books.

Coster, J.S. & Schwebel, M. (1997). Well-functioning in professional psychologists. *Professional Psychology: Research and Practice, 28*, 5-13.

Cushway, D. (1996). Tolerance begins at home: Implications for counselor training. *International Journal for the Advancement of Counseling, 18*, 189-197.

Faunce, P.S. (1990). Self-care and wellness of feminist therapists. In H. Lerman & N. Porter (Eds.), *Feminist ethics in psychotherapy* (pp. 123-130). New York: Springer Publishing Company.

Feminist Therapy Institute. (1990). Feminist Therapy Institute Code of Ethics. In H. Lerman & N. Porter (Eds.), *Feminist ethics in psychotherapy* (pp. 37-40). New York: Springer.

Gilroy, P., Carroll, L., & Murra, J. (1998). Does depression affect clinical practice: A national survey of women psychotherapists. Poster session presented at the annual meeting of the American Psychological Association, San Francisco, CA.

Guy, J.D., Poelstra, P.L., & Stark, M.J. (1989). Personal distress and therapeutic effectiveness: National survey of psychologists practicing psychotherapy. *Professional Psychology: Research and Practice, 20*, 48-50.

Kramen-Kahn, B., & Hansen, N. D. (1998). Rafting the rapids: Occupational hazards, rewards, and coping strategies of psychotherapists. *Professional Psychology: Research and Practice, 29*, 130-134.

Mahoney, M.J. (1997). Psychotherapists' personal problems and self-care patterns. *Professional Psychology: Research and Practice, 28*, 14-16.

Margison, F. (1997). Stress and psychotherapy: An overview. In V.P. Varma (Ed.), *Stress in psychotherapists* (pp. 210-234). London: Routledge.

Moursand, J. (1993). *The process of counseling and therapy* (3rd ed.), Englewood Cliffs, New Jersey: Prentice Hall.

Nathan, P.E. (1986). Unanswered questions about distressed professionals. In R.R. Kilburg, P.E. Nathan, & R.W. Thoreson (Eds.), *Professionals in distress: Issues, syndromes and solutions in psychology* (pp. 27-36). Washington, D.C.: American Psychological Association.

Norcross, J.C., Strausser-Kirtland, D., & Missar, D.C. (1988). The process and outcomes of psychotherapists' personal treatment experiences. *Psychotherapy, 25*, 36-43.

Norman, J., & Rosvall, S. (1994). Help-seeking behavior among mental health practitioners. *Clinical Social Work Journal, 22*, 449-460.

Pope, K.S. & Tabachnick, B.G. (1994). Therapists as patients: A national survey of psychologists' experiences, problems, and beliefs. *Professional Psychology: Research and Practice, 25*, 247-258.

Pope, K.S., Tabachnick, B.G., & Keith-Speigel, P. (1987). Ethics in practice: The beliefs and behaviors of psychologists as therapists. *American Psychologist, 42*, 993-1006.

Porter, N. (1995). Therapist self-care: A proactive ethical approach. In H. Lerman & N. Porter (Eds.), *Feminist ethics in psychotherapy* (pp. 247-266). New York: Springer Publishing Company.

Prochaska, J.O. & Norcross, J.C. (1983). Psychotherapists' perspectives on treating themselves and their clients for psychic distress. *Professional Psychology: Research and Practice, 14*, 642-655.

Ross, W.D. (1930). *The right and the good*. Oxford, England: Clarendon Press.

Schwebel, M., & Coster, J. (1998). Well-functioning in professional psychologists: As program heads see it. *Professional Psychology: Research and Practice, 29*, 284-292.

Sherman, M.D. (1996). Distress and professional impairment due to mental health problems among psychotherapists. *Clinical Psychology Review, 16*, 299-315.

Sherman, M.D., & Thelen, M.H. (1998). Distress and professional impairment among psychologists in clinical practice. *Professional Psychology: Research and Practice, 29*, 79-85.

Solomon, R.S. (1984). *Ethics: A brief introduction*. New York: McGraw-Hill.

Stoltenberg, C. (1981). Approaching supervision from a developmental perspective: The counselor complexity model. *Journal of Counseling Psychology, 28*, 59-65.

Sussman, M.B. (1995). *A perilous calling. The hazards of psychotherapy practice*. New York: John Wiley & Sons, Inc.

Walsh, S., Nichols, K. & Cormack, M. (1991). Self-care and clinical psychologists: A threatening obligation? *Clinical Psychology Forum, 37*, 5-7.

Wood, B.J., Klein, S., Cross, H.J., Lammers, C.J., & Elliott, J.K. (1985). Impaired practitioners: Psychologists' opinions about prevalence, and proposals for intervention. *Professional Psychology: Research and Practice, 16*, 843-850.

Index

Abrams, J. Z., 58
Abuse disorder, 26
Abuse of power, in psychological diagnosis, 24,25,32
Adolescents and children
  empowerment of, 4
  See also Child welfare system psychotherapy, moral directions in; Children's growth and development; Family therapy, goal vs. parental responsibility
Agendas, in child welfare system psychotherapy, 58,59
American Psychological Association (APA), 77
  ethics code and, 77,124,125
Americans with Disabilities Act, 88,93
Anderson, G., 54
Anorexia. *See* Eating disorders
APA (American Psychological Association), 77,124,125
Appearance norms, lesbians and, 30-31,35

Ballou, Mary, 33
Berson, Nancy, 34
Bion, W., 18
Bloom, Alexandra, 4,7-19
Body image
  feminists and, 29-31
  heterosexual females and, 29-32
  lesbian-feminists and, 29-32
Bordo, Susan, 36
Brown, Laura S., 78,138
Bruner, J. S., 17
Bruns, Cindy M., 4,69-85
Bulimia. *See* Eating disorders
Burke, W.F., 10

Carroll, Lynne, 4,133
Cartledge, Sue, 35
Case examples
  of client advocacy vs. institutional power, 47-48
  of community mental health, 45-48
  of empowerment vs. confidentiality, 45-47
  of moral decision points, 48-50, 60-62
  of suicide prevention, 42-45
  of therapist as interpreter, 64-67
  of therapist as "Loyal" expert, 62-64
  See also Family therapy, goal vs. parental responsibility; Feminist therapy, morality and responsibility
Child abuse
  family therapy and, 118,119
  feminist therapist and, 26
  See also Family therapy, goal vs. parental responsibility
Child welfare system psychotherapy, moral directions in
  agendas and, 58,59
  background on, 55
  conclusions, 67-68
  confidentiality and, 54,59,60-61
  crisis interventions and, 57
  empowerment and, 54, 61
  ethical guidelines and, 59
  family relationships and, 56,58
  fragmentation and, 53,55,56,57,60, 63,64,66
  growth and development and, 55
  integrity and, 53,58,59,60,63,67
  loss and dislocation and, 56,61-62
  moral decision points case example, 60-62

confidentiality and, 60-61
dysfunctional family and, 61-62
therapist as advocate and, 61-62
moral dilemmas and, 53,54,55, 56,61
moral dimensions of, 58-59
oppression and, 59,60
relationships and, 54
religious guidelines and, 58
resources and, 56
socio-economic issues and, 55
summary regarding, 53
systemic sources of, 57
therapist as interpreter case example, 64-67
family conflicts and, 64-67
sexual abuse victim and, 64
therapist as "Loyal" expert case example, 62-64
identity formation and learning in crisis, 63
maturation factors and, 63-64
recommendations and, 62
therapist role in, 57,59
truth, lies and bureaucracy, 64-67
truth and complexity, 64
Childhood development, parent child relationship and, 17
Children. *See* Adolescents and children; Child welfare system psychotherapy, moral directions in; Children's growth and development; Family therapy, goal vs. parental responsibility
Children's growth and development, child welfare system psychotherapy and, 55
Childs, E., 72-73
Chodorow, N., 11
Classism, 22
Client advocacy
community mental health, feminist dilemmas in, 42,51
disabled clients and, psychotherapy of, 87

vs. institutional power, 47-48
Client empowerment
community mental health, feminist dilemmas in, 40,42,51
See also Empowerment
Codes of ethics, community mental health, feminist dilemmas in, 41-42
Community mental health, feminist dilemmas in
client advocacy and, 42,51
client empowerment and, 40,42,51
codes of ethics and, 41-42
conflict case examples and
client advocacy vs. institutional power, 47-48
identity development vs. confidentiality, 45-47
moral responsibility vs. confidentiality, 48-51
suicide prevention vs. self-determination, 42-45
institutionalized power and, 40, 50-51
moral guidance systems and, 39-40
power differentials and, 41-42, 50-51
religious framework and, 41
self-determination focus of, 41
summary regarding, 21,50-51
Confidentiality
vs. identity development, 45-47
vs. moral responsibility, 48-50
Conflict case examples, 45-48
Conoley, J. C., 130
Contextual issues, feminist psychotherapy, women in prison, 70,72
Cormack, M., 141
Countertransference, 9-10,11,12,17, 94-95,126-127
Cushway, D., 140

Demoralization, 13
Depression, 14
Developmental theory, 11

Diagnosis abuses, in mental health system, 24,25,32
Diagnostic and Statistical Manual of Mental Disorders (DSM), 24
Disabled clients. *See* Psychotherapy, disabled clients and
Doherty, W. J., 59,108
Dominant culture
   feminist naming and, 21,22,25, 27,34
   moral paradigm of, 21,22,23,25,26, 27,28,34
   morality and, 21,23,25,26,27,28,34
Dominant heterosexual culture. *See* Dominant culture
Dominant meaning system, 16
Dominant power structure, 25
DSM-II (Diagnostic and Statistical Manual of Mental Disorders), 24
DSM-IV (Diagnostic and Statistical Manual of Mental Disorders), 24

Eating disorders
   heterosexual females and, 29-31
   lesbian feminists and, 29-31
Empowerment
   adolescents and children and, 4
   agencies or systems and, 4
   feminist morality and, 35
   feminist naming tool of, 21
   feminist principle of, 4
   suicide prevention case example and, 42-45
Empowerment vs. confidentiality case example, 45-47
Epistemology
   contemporary, 11-12
   ethical code and, 3
   feminist critiques of, 10-11
   models of, 8-10
   training in, 3
Erickson, R., 108

Ethical code, 3
Ethical issues, 16

Family therapy, goal vs. parental responsibility, 117
   case example of, 119-124
      abusive relationship history and, 120
      child custody through therapy focus and, 119
      conclusion regarding, 130
      confidentiality maintenance, child custody, 123,124-125
      developmentally challenged children and, 120
      dysfunctional family history and, 120
      feminist therapy considerations and, 128-130
      hypervigilance and distrust of others and, 121
      impulsive anger and depression therapy focus and, 121
      interactions with children, 122
      legal and ethical guidelines, 124-125
      morality and, 128
      oppression history and, 121
      parenting skills focus and, 122
      PTSD and major depression diagnosis and, 120
      therapeutic considerations, 125-127
      transference and countertransference, 126-127
   child abuse and, 118,119
   child custody and, 118,119
   family reunification and, 118
   feminist perspective and, 119
   morality and ethics and, 119
   social awareness and, 118
   therapist conflicting guidelines and, 118-119
"Family values" concept, 23
Female heterosexuality, patriarchy and, 28-29

Feminism, feminists, 2
  body image obsession and, 29-31
  empowerment and, 4
  gender inequities and, 22
  See also Community mental health, feminist dilemmas in; Feminist morality; Feminist naming; Feminist psychotherapy, women in prison; Feminist therapist; Feminist therapy; Feminist therapy, morality and responsibility
Feminist morality
  empowerment and, 35
  naming within, 36
  oppression and, 34,36
  as social control mechanism, 23
  See also Feminist therapy, morality and responsibility
Feminist naming
  dominant culture and, 21,22,25,27,34
  empowerment tool of, 21,26
  oppression and, 26
  social impact of, 25,26
Feminist psychotherapy, women in prison
  complexities of, 72-78
  contextual issues of, 70,72
  definition of terms and, 71
  dominant culture morality and, 73
  dual allegiance of therapists in, 76-78
  dual alliance of therapists in, 70-71
  emotional vulnerability and, 74
  empowerment and, 77
  institutional oppressions and, 71-72
  invisibility of, 70,75
  naming and, 72
  oppression and the therapeutic relationship, 74-76
  population trends and, 70
  practical applications and, 78-84
    challenges and opportunities and, 78
    client empowerment and, 80,82
    client's beliefs and realities and, 80
    confidentiality and, 79
    cultural factors and, 81-82
    ethical guidelines and, 79,83,84
    informed consent and, 79
    interpersonal trauma survival and, 80
    moral principles and, 79,83,84
    peer support and, 79
    policy creation and implementation, 83
    power issues and, 80,82,84
    self-examination and, 78
    self-image and, 81
    social and political forces and, 79
    staff education and, 82-83
    therapist roles and, 79,82,83,84
    therapist-client relationship and, 79
    women of color and, 81,83
  psychological treatment opportunities for, 70
  racial oppression and, 73
  self-determination and autonomy, 75
  women of color and, 70,72
Feminist therapist
  childhood abuse and, 26
  feminist perspective and, 36
  lesbian-feminist morality and, 32,34,35
  naming and, 32-34
  power and, 33-34
  See also Community mental health, feminist dilemmas in; Feminist therapy, morality and responsibility
Feminist therapy, 1,4,10,11
  goals of, 33,34
  See also Feminist therapy, morality and responsibility
Feminist Therapy Institute, ethical code of, 4,36,59,71,72,77,129,134,139
Feminist therapy, morality and responsibility

case example 1
  family commitments and, 110
  family vs. personal responsibility, 109,112
  family unit obligation and, 110-111
  Holocaust survivors and, 109
case example 2
  dependence and, 112
  family origins and, 112-113
  lack of intimacy and, 112
  marriage dissatisfaction and, 112-113
  moral belief system and, 113
  role of therapy in, 112-113
discussion, 113-114
  decisionmaking process and, 114
  ethics and, 114
  improvement of self and, 114
  individual's belief system and, 114
  intra- and interpersonal conflicts and, 114
ethics defined and, 106, 107
individual and social interests
  abusive situations and, 107-108
  ethical belief system and, 108
  individual moral code and, 108
  morality issues and, 108
  psychotherapy and, moral discourse in, 108
  self care advocacy and, 107-108
  therapist as role model and, 107
  women and oppression, 107
morality defined and, 106,107, 108-109
personal belief system and, 106
Ten Commandments vs. Golden Rule and, 106-107
See also Feminist morality
Freud, Sigmund, 8-10
  on countertransference, 9,10
  on positivism, 9
  on purpose of science, 9
  on reality, 9
  on relativity, 9
  on truth, 9
Frye, Marilyn, 28-29

Gender issues
  inequities and, 22,25
  lesbian-feminist morality and, 28
  psychological diagnoses and, 24,25
Gilligan, C., 11
Gilroy, Paula J., 4,133

Havel, Vaclav, 13
Henry, Jay, 80
Herman, J. L., 15-16
Heteropatriarchal oppression, 28-29
Heterosexual females
  body image and, 29-32
  eating disorders and, 29-31
Hoagland, Sara Lucia, 35
Hoffman, I. Z., 11-12
Homophobia, 22,27
Hooks, Bell, 76

ICD (International Classification of Diseases), 24
Institutional power
  vs. client advocacy case example, 47-48
  community mental health, feminist dilemmas in, 40,50-51
  oppression and, 23,36
International Classification of Diseases (ICD), 24

Kaschak, Ellyn, 1-5
Keller, E. F., 10-11
Keller, Sally, 4,117
Kibel, Sharla, 4,53-68
Kitzinger, Celia, 34
"Knowing"
  genesis of, 17-19
  moral accountability and, 13,18

psychotherapy and, 7,8,11,13,15, 16
See also Psychotherapy, moral accountability and
Kristiansen, Connie M., 80

Larson, P., 130
Legal requirements, 48-51
Leibowitz, N., 58
Lemas, P., 108
Lesbian identity, 28
Lesbian-feminism
   body image and, 30
   eating disorders and, 29-31
   group norms and, 22,26,27
   morality and, 26,27-28,34-35
   naming and, 22,23,26-28,35
   oppression and, 28-29
   "rules" of, 21,23,28-29, 30-32,34-36
   sexual practices and, 29
   woman-centered environment and, 22,27
Lesbian-feminist morality
   casualties of
      physical appearance and, 29-32, 35
      sexual desire/behavior and, 28-29,35
      summary regarding, 31-32
   enforcement of, 34
   gender issues and, 28
Lesbian-separatist, 28
Lesko, Teresa M., 4,69-85
Linton, S., 88
London, P., 108
Loss and dislocation, child welfare system
   psychotherapy and, 56,61-62

Mainstream diagnostic paradigm, 26
Mania, 14
Margison, F., 139
Mental health system
   diagnosis abuses in, 24,25,32
   See also Community mental health, feminist dilemmas in
Moral guidance systems. *See* Community mental health, feminist dilemmas in
Moral issues, dilemmas, accountability. *See* Child welfare system psychotherapy, moral directions in; Feminist psychotherapy, women in prison; Feminist therapy; Moral paradigm; Morality; Psychotherapy, moral accountability and
Moral paradigm
   dominant culture and, 21,22,23, 25,26,27-28,34
   dominant culture in, 22,25
   society and, 23,25
Morality
   dominant culture and, 21,23,25,26, 27,28, 34
   emotional growth and, 8
   "Family values" and, 23
   feminist naming and, 4,23,25
   framework of, 35
   lesbian-feminist casualties and, 28-29
   lesbian-feminist "rules" and, 4,27, 28,36
   "golden rule" of, 13,14
   in therapeutic practice, 4,5
   See also feminist therapy, morality and responsibility; Psychotherapy, moral accountability and
Morality of the soul, concept of, 106
Murra, Jennifer, 4,133

Naming
   classism and, 26
   dominant culture and, 21,22,25,34
   empowerment tool of, 21,26,33
   feminist moral framework and, 36

feminist therapists and, 32-34
heteropatriarchal oppression and, 28-29
homophobia and, 26,27
legitimacy and validation of, 25
lesbian-feminist community and, 22,23
lesbian-separatism and, 28
negative impact of, 26
politics of, 21-36
power of, 25,33
racism and, 26
sexism and, 26
social impact of, 25,26
tool for women's experience, 33
See also Feminist naming
Narcissism, 14
Nicholas, M., 108
Nichols, K., 141

Olkin, Rhoda, 87
Oppression
    in child welfare system psychotherapy, 59,60
    classism and, 22
    feminist morality and, 34,36
    homophobia and, 22,27
    institutional power and, 23,36
    lesbians and, 28-29
    racism and, 22

Parent child relationship, 17
Parental responsibility. *See* family therapy, goal vs. parental responsibility
Pathological identity, transgendered individuals and, 24,25
Patriarchy, female heterosexuality and, 28-29
Perkins, Rachel, 34
Philosophy, 3
Pitman, Gayle E., 21-38
Politics of naming
    traditional vs. feminist, 23-27

See also Naming
Pope, K. S., 134-135
Porter, N., 134,135
Post traumatic stress disorder (PTSD), 26,120
Postmodernist philosophers, 9,11
Power differentials, community mental health, feminist dilemmas in, 41-42,50-51
Prilleltensky, I., 107
Psychoanalytic theory
    epistemology models of, 8
    Freud and, 8-10
Psychological diagnoses
    abuse of power in, 24,25,32
    gender issues and, 24,25
Psychology
    ethical practice in, 32-34
    feminists in, 11, 32-34
    naming in, 24,25,32-34
    See also Feminist therapy, morality and responsibility
Psychosis, 14
Psychotherapy
    ethical issues and, 2,3,4,16
    gender issues and, 10,11,22,24,25
    moral issues and, 1,2,3,7,12
    as political act, 2
    therapeutic dyad in, 12,17
    therapist role in, 14,15
    training and education in, 2,3, 59,140
    See also Child welfare system psychotherapy, moral directions in; family therapy, goal vs. parental responsibility; feminist therapy, morality and responsibility; women psychotherapists, self-care as a moral imperative
Psychotherapy, disabled clients and, 4, 87-102
    advocacy and, 87
    case example of, 100-102
    conclusions regarding, 102

disability culture and, 87
disability-affirmative therapy and, 87,88,89
disability and impairment, defined, 89
as minority group, 88
minority model, treatment implications of, 87
psychology and, 88-89
therapist's responsibilities and case formulation, 95-96
competence, 96
countertransference, 94-95
dialectics, 93-94
disability context and, 97-98
disability vs. impairment, 92
disability as minority, 90-91
disability as part of diversity, 98
models of disability, 91-92
personal aspects of, 89-90
political aspects of, 90
professional aspects of, 90
research, 99-100
sociopolitical, 94
systems, 97
teaching, 98-99
values, 92-93
valuing disability culture, 91
Psychotherapy, moral accountability and clinical implications of
patient trauma and, 15
safety issues and, 14-15
self-confrontation and, 15,16
therapist resistance and, 15,16
demoralization and
psychic survival and, 13-14
psychopathology and, 14
epistemology, feminist critiques of
developmental concepts and, 11
gender bias and, 10
moral decisions by women and, 11
"neutral" analytic observer concept and, 10-11
epistemology models and
Freud on postmodernism, 9
Freud on purpose of science and, 9
Freud's psychoanalytic theory and, 8-9
knowing and, 8
genesis of knowing and
childhood development and, 17
parent child relationships and, 17
patient resistance and, 17,18
self-confrontation and, 19
therapist countertransference and, 17
therapist resistance and, 17,18
therapist self understanding and, 17
psychoanalytic epistemology and
countertransference and, 11-12
"knowing" and, 11
summary regarding, 7-8
PTSD (post traumatic stress disorder), 26,120

Racism, 22
Reik, T., 15,18,19
Religious framework
child welfare system psychotherapy and, 58
community mental health, feminist dilemmas in, 41
Ross, W. D., 134
Rothblum, Esther, 30

Schuchman, K. M., 54
Self-determination
community mental health focus of, 41
See also Empowerment
Self-identity, 45-47
Sexuality
and physical appearance, 21,28-29, 30-32,34-36
See also Lesbian-feminism, *specific subject*
Sherman, M. D., 135
Society, moral framework of, 23,25

Socio-economic issues, child welfare system
  psychotherapy and, 55
Solberg, M. M., 13,16
Solomon, R. S., 134
Stern, D., 17,18
Suicide prevention, vs. self-determination case example, 42-45

Tabachnick, B. G., 134-135
Tansey, M. J., 10
Telushkin, J., 58
Thelen, M. H., 135
Therapeutic dyad, 12,17
Training
  epistemology and, 3
  psychotherapy and, 2,3,59,140
Transference, 11,12,126-127
  See also Countertransference
Transgendered individuals, pathological identity and, 24,25
Transsexuals. *See* Transgendered individuals

Walsh, S., 141
Warwick, Lynda, 4
Wasserstrom, R., 16
Weiner, Kayla Miriyam, 4,105
Woman-centered environment, lesbians and, 22,27
Women, feminist belief system and, 22
Women in prison
  feminist psychotherapy and, 69-85
  See also Feminist psychotherapy, women in prison
Women psychotherapists, self-care as a moral imperative, 133
  conclusion regarding, 141-142
  distress and impairment among practitioners, 134-135
  impairment and commitment to self-care awareness and, 137-139
  impairment defined, 135
  professional recommendations regarding, 139-141
  self-care and
    activities of, 135-136
    defined, 135-136
    depression among practitioners and, 134-135
    guidelines for, 134
    instruction in, 140
    problems in, 136-137
Wright, B. A., 95